SELF-DISCIPLINE

Simple Daily Habits And Exercises To Develop Mental Toughness, Beat Procrastination And Achieve Goals For Success In Life

by Daniel Cooper

Copyright and Liability Disclaimer

First Published in 2020.

Copyright © 2020 Daniel Cooper

is engaged in rendering legal, accounting, or other professional services by publishing this book. As each individual situation is unique, questions relevant to self-discipline and specific to the individual should be addressed to an appropriate professional to ensure that the situation has been evaluated carefully and appropriately. The author and publisher specifically disclaim any liability, loss, or risk which is incurred as a consequence, directly or indirectly, of the use and application of any of the contents of this work.

TABLE OF CONTENTS

INTRODUCTION

There is one important to understand about self-discipline: the harder is the work on it and the more you apply yourself to self-improvement, the greater your accomplishments and better your relationships.

What you are getting out of life is a straight reflection of what you have put into it. That is why the most successful people today are actually those who have taken control of their destiny: people who have created a plan and followed through with perseverance and diligence. People who have applied themselves to self-discipline.

On the path of success, you will discover that everyone has a different view of self-discipline. While self-discipline may mean meeting a professional target to some, to others it is curbing a bad habit. No matter your definition, you alone can work toward a successful life.

To me, self-discipline means possessing a can-do attitude that says, "I might fail, but that won't make me a failure." That conviction came in handy during hard times. Those times I found it hard to see any light at the end of the tunnel, my positive attitude saw me through.

In this book, be prepared to embrace the vision and understand what you desire out of life. Be prepared to create a positive mindset and learning from mistakes instead of making excuses or giving up. Be prepared to steadfastly focus on your goals and meet roadblocks ahead.

CHAPTER 1

What Is Self-Discipline

According to author M.R. Kopmeyer, "Self-discipline is the ability to make yourself do what you should do when you should do it, whether you feel like it or not."

Regardless of your skillset and expertise, you will not get far if you do not cultivate the art of self-discipline. You have to do the necessary things even when you don't feel like doing them, especially when you don't feel like doing them. No matter where you are at in life, you should hold yourself to a system that checks your excesses and keeps you in line.

"I don't just feel like it" has always been the major reason for procrastination. But if we keep waiting until we "feel like it" to come to action, we're in trouble.

Self-discipline can be explained in different ways. It could mean endurance, restraint, thinking before acting, perseverance, or carrying out your plans and decisions despite obstacles, hardships or inconvenience. Self-discipline could mean self-control, too. This simply means avoiding unhealthy excesses which may have negative repercussions.

Whatever definition you fancy, one thing stands out about self-discipline: that innate ability to forgo instant pleasure and gratification in favor of more satisfying results or greater gain, even though it takes time and effort.

I have found that the term self-discipline carries a feeling of dread in many people. They see it as resistance and discomfort—something difficult to reach, nasty, requiring a great deal of sacrifice and effort. But this is quite the opposite. You can attain and exercise without having to undergo immense suffering.

Contrary to popular belief, real self-discipline is never punishing or restrictive of your lifestyle. It does not mean living like a monk or being narrow-minded. The truth is that self-discipline comes from a place of staying power and inner strength needed to manage life's everyday affairs while reaching your life goals.

By adopting a spirit of self-discipline, I have been able to overcome indecisiveness, procrastination, and laziness, which used to be the major challenges I faced. I saw myself taking bold actions and persevering with them, even though those actions seem demanding and unpleasant. I saw myself applying moderation in things I do. In the process, I became more considerate, understanding, tolerant and patient. For someone like me who was prone to bend easily to external influence and pressure, I began to take more control of my life. I saw myself not just setting goals but taking concrete steps to reach them. I became more punctual, putting more time and effort into the most important things in my life. I was exercising regularly, avoiding alcohol and drugs, stopped procrastinating and began to save for retirement.

Self-discipline comes with mastering your thoughts. By controlling what you think, you can control how you act. It comes with doing things when you don't want to. It comes with being free from weakness and laziness, being free from doubt and fear, and being from the demands and expectations of others.

<u>Overall, the core truths of self-discipline are</u>:

1.   Perseverance.

2.   Not giving up in spite of setbacks and failure.

3.   Self-control of one's conduct, desires, and feelings

4.   Resisting temptations or distractions.

5.   Trying repeatedly until your goals are accomplished.

6.   Doing the necessary things first.

Understand that the path to success is filled with a myriad of challenges. Getting there won't be easy. But if you can harness self-discipline (persistence + perseverance), like how I will show you in this book, you will rise above whatever problem and then live a happy and satisfied life.

Asides loss and failure in life, a lack of self-discipline can cause health and relationship problems. A lack of self-discipline can even be traced to addictions and eating disorders.

Every day, you are faced with several decisions to make. Self-discipline is the only factor that allows you to make the decision that is most favorable in the long term—forgoing instant gratification. Instead of picking the most pleasurable or comfortable decision, you withstand that temptation, because you understand that the attractiveness of the easiest solution is only fleeting.

Therefore, when you are self-disciplined, you find yourself thinking long-term instead of short-term. You know that these "comfortable" decisions would never lead you to success.

But the problem here is that each pleasure-based decision often does not immediately impact your life negatively. But when combined, these unprofitable little decisions can be dangerous.

Mental strength

We cannot talk about self-discipline without first understanding something called "mental strength." A lot of mental strength is required to control your desires, feelings, and behaviors. Keeping things under control involves addressing the most important things first while doing away with distractions. Gaining mental strength is never easy—but it is possible.

Having the essential willpower needed to do what needs to be done and having that innate ability to withstand temptations to achieve long-term goals all require mental strength.

Why is self-discipline so hard

One major factor that makes self-discipline look hard is our comfort zone. We love our comfort zone and we will often do anything to remain there even it means remaining stagnant in life.

The core value of a disciplined mind, however, says you should do things, whether they are pleasurable or not. As humans, we constantly quest for pleasure and in the process miss out on our long-term goals. Instead of focusing on the end reward, we are scared of the pain and effort required to make our dreams come true.

Another factor that negatively affects self-discipline is the spirit of entitled expectations. We are not prepared to continuously push ourselves. We want things to be easy. To work out smoothly for us. We expect life to give us the best because we "deserve" the best. We shrink away whenever we encounter problems.

Also, self-discipline is not inborn. You can develop, strengthen and exercise it. Just like working out or building muscles. However, most of us find this building process to be quite difficult. So we accept failure and settle for mediocrity. If you can live with the prospect of failing, maintain self-discipline is impossible.

A life without purpose is a life without discipline. When you don't have a vision for your life, how can you maintain discipline? Likewise, temptations are the bane of humanity. We are tempted every second of the day. Binge eating, money, alcohol, smoking, sex, drugs, laziness and so on. Each day we give in to these temptations and enter a vicious circle of negative habits. Without the willpower to withstand temptations, we become slaves to our vices.

Building the muscle of self-discipline

Just like an athlete builds muscles through regular exercise, you too can build self-discipline. This process is a continuous one. If you don't continue to build your muscles, they will deteriorate. The same thing goes for self-discipline. The more you exercise it into every aspect of your life, the stronger you become. Then it becomes a vital part of you.

The key thing here is starting small when building your self-discipline muscle. Overdoing anything is a killer of motivation. By starting small, you give yourself time to get used to this new behavior. Then, you can gradually raise the exertion of your self-discipline muscle

In building self-discipline, concentration is important. Often, we get too thrilled about the big picture or the future that we fail to concentrate on the present. Follow your goals one step at a time. Distractions will always come; it is your responsibility to tune them out if you truly want to succeed. Start small and work your way up—never lose that momentum.

Pick out one area of your life where you would like to be disciplined. It could be going to bed early and waking up on time or reducing your beer consumption or reading a book for an hour every day.

After mastering discipline in one aspect of your life, you can then move on to the next aspect. Self-discipline can become a habit if you're ready to put in work to establish it.

Most people understand the benefits of self-discipline, but very few truly work on how to grow and toughen it. In this book, you will be provided the necessary guidance and information, guidance for growing your self-discipline—a skill everyone needs for achieving success.

CHAPTER 2

The Science And Psychology Of Self-Discipline

Self-discipline is the factor that tells you to save instead of splurging now. It is that factor that helps you keep your head down, work and study when you actually do not feel like it, to earn that promotion or degree. Self-discipline lets you say no to that tempting third glass of whiskey, extra dessert, or cigarette. It tells you to jump on that treadmill. Self-discipline helps keep your eyes on your goals.

That is why psychological scientists have looked at self-discipline for many years—to identify who is self-controlled under what conditions—and why. What goes on in our head (brain's neurons and cognitive machinery) when we give in to temptation or say no?

Psychological scientist's view of self-discipline

Psychological scientists define self-discipline as the ability to delay gratification—resist short-term temptations to accomplish long-term goals. It is the ability to remove an unwanted impulse, feeling or thought. It is also the capacity to use a "cool" cognitive system of behavior instead of a "hot" emotional one.

Psychological scientists also define self-discipline as a mindful, effort-based regulation of the self by the self. Self-discipline is also seen as a limited resource that can be exhausted.

Self-discipline is studied to provide treatments for addiction, help people make healthy lifestyle choices, like avoiding substance abuse, exercising and eating well. Scientists have identified that a high level of self-discipline is strongly connected to life satisfaction. Studies have also shown that people with high levels of self-discipline are in general cheerier, healthier and wealthier.

Numerous studies have shown that the emotional, motivational, cognitive, and metabolic aspects of our lives can be boosted with self-discipline. To address the problems our society is currently facing (addition and obesity, for instance), thousands of studies have been done on self-discipline and how it works.

According to one survey by the American Psychological Association about making healthy lifestyle changes, participants mostly cite a lack of self-discipline as a major factor holding them back from changing for the better. While a lack of self-discipline negatively affects lives, science says self-discipline can be learned. And through practice, it can be strengthened.

However, the barrier to your goals is not just a lack of self-discipline. To achieve your goals, you must first know your motivation for change and establish a clear goal. Next, start observing your behavior toward that goal. The third and final aspect is self-discipline. Whether your goal is to spend less time on social media, study more, stop smoking or lose weight, science says that you must first make the commitment and resist short-term temptations to achieve long-term goals.

When it comes to academics, researchers have found that students with high self-discipline have better school attendance, better grades, score higher on standardized tests, better relationship skills, less alcohol abuse, and binge eating, higher self-esteem, and are more likely to be admitted to a competitive high school or college programs. To even predict academic success, self-discipline is said to be more vital than IQ.

Overall, studies have shown that individuals with high self-discipline in childhood will grow into adults with greater mental and physical health, better financial security and savings attitude, and fewer criminal convictions and substance-abuse problems. Those patterns are even true for children with different intelligence levels, home lives, and socioeconomic status.

Delayed gratification

Delayed gratification can be seen in an ex-smoker forfeiting the enjoyment of a cigarette to avoid an increased chance of lung cancer later on and experience good health. It is seen in a shopper resisting the urge to splurge at the mall to save for a comfortable retirement.

The hot and cool system

A school of thought believes that the "hot-and-cool" system explains why we succeed or fail at self-discipline. The nature of the cool system is cognitive. It is fundamentally a thinking system, combining knowledge about your goals, actions, feelings, and sensations—jogging your memory, for instance, why you should not smoke a cigarette.

Unlike the reflective cool system, the hot system is emotional and impulsive. The hot system is in charge of your fast, kneejerk responses to specific triggers—like smoking a cigarette or splurging in the mall without being thoughtful of the long-term consequences. In cartoon analogy, the hot system is the devil on your shoulder while the cool system is the angel. Self-discipline fails when you the "hot" stimulus basically dominate the cool system—this then causes impetuous actions.

Brain activity

While examining brain activity with functional magnetic resonance imaging, scientists found that when presented with tempting stimuli, subjects with high self-discipline will show brain patterns different from those with low self-discipline. The prefrontal cortex (a region controlling executive functions, like choice making) is more active in people with higher self-discipline. And the ventral striatum (region processing rewards and desires) is more active in those with lower self-discipline.

The theory of self-discipline as a limited resource

The theory of self-discipline depletion says your self-discipline depletes the more you exert it. From resisting the urge to eat a burger and settling for a salad to biting your tongue when you want to make a snide remark to studying instead of checking Facebook—a rising body of research think it can take a mental toll when you continue to resist temptations. A muscle getting weary from overuse.

Depleting events happen in everyday social interactions that require self-discipline. Whether it's willing yourself to smile through your mother-in –law's prolonged visit, or forcing yourself to be tactful with an annoying co-worker, research says maintaining relationships and interacting with people can drain your self-discipline.

The energy model of self-control

One explanation some scientists follow is a theory called "the energy model of self-control." This model says your brain can be likened to a muscle with a limited supply of energy which can be exhausted via exertion. No human on earth is always disciplined; there will always be lapses. And this energy model says these lapses happen when one act of self-discipline deteriorates your resolve (willpower to be disciplined), leaving you "drained" as you face another challenge.

In this model, self-discipline is dependent on carbohydrate metabolism. The more you exert self-disciple, the more you exhaust stored carbohydrates in your body. So this school of thought believes that the lesser the carbohydrate in your system, the harder it is to be self-disciplined. However, many other researchers have found no evidence connecting carbohydrate metabolism and self-discipline.

Although muscles become fatigued by exercise in the short term, they can be toughened by steady exercise in the long term. Likewise, repeatedly exerting self-discipline can increase your self-discipline muscle. By flexing your self-discipline strength, you can build it over time.

Don't rush it

Scientists have recognized self-discipline as a major constituent of healthy lifestyle choices. Unfortunately, in our goal for a happier and healthier life, we make straining decisions to resist impulses each day. Our willpower is put to a test almost every hour. Research has connected a lack of self-discipline as a barrier to maintaining a healthy weight. For instance, children with better self-discipline were less likely to become obese as adolescents, because of their capacity to delay gratification or delay gratification.

However, research says rushing your goals at once is not a smart thing to do. For example, don't try to begin a new workout plan, adopt a healthy diet and quit smoking at the same time. A smarter approach is to take your goals one by one. Once you have one good habit in place, it becomes routine, and your self-discipline no longer feels depleted. With clear goals, proper self-monitoring and some practice, training your self-discipline to withstand temptation is possible.

CHAPTER 3

The Difference Between Conventional Discipline And Self-Discipline

The word "discipline" is from the Latin word "*disciplina*" which means instruction or teaching. Modern definitions have added punishment to discipline; however, the original meaning was never about punishment, but rather teaching to improve behavior or gain a skill.

Conventional discipline is borne out of external rules and laws. This kind of discipline is needed to make sure that all social frameworks and laws are obeyed. For many of us, we follow conventional discipline because we are aware of the punishment higher authorities (boss, judge, or police, for instance) can dish out when we go astray.

Conventional (external) discipline is often ruled by fear. For example, if a man driven by conventional discipline were guaranteed that he could break the law without facing any consequences, he would most likely do so. This is seen in drivers who deliberately and constantly neglect speed limits when no speed enforcement is around.

Conventional discipline is found in homes and schools. It is easily taught to us from childhood to adulthood. Our parents enforce conventional discipline when we do something wrong. And reward us for following their rules. As adults, our professor, boss, and the government enforce external discipline. Therefore, this kind of external discipline is based on a reward and punishment system. These become the motivating factor.

Self-discipline (or internal discipline), however, is a much-refined form of discipline in which your self-control is not motivated by the possibility of external punishment. With self-discipline, you are in total control of your behavior and mindset. You are not controlled by fear. Your discipline and behavior remain firm whether there is a treat of external punishment or not. You are self-governed, following your accepted internal law.

Self-discipline, unlike conventional discipline, operated with a disciplined internal code. One that withstands temptation. Sadly, we live in a world where self-discipline is low in many. We do not strive for good nutrition or sufficient exercise. We are held up by the Internet and social media—when there is work to be done. For people with low levels of self-discipline rely on external factors to maintain discipline. They need a figure of authority to assert discipline over themselves; they will not succeed unless they have someone to which they can be accountable.

Unlike conventional discipline which is easily taught, it is more difficult to teach self-discipline. You can encourage self-discipline in someone but can never enforce it. You can never threaten anyone into self-discipline. Additionally, self-discipline stands out from conventional discipline because you are ultimately in charge of your own actions and they have a responsibility to yourself and others.

Self-discipline gives you the freedom to make informed decisions concerning whatever you do. It is a personal choice and cannot be forced. In fact, external discipline cannot produce self-disciplined people.

If you are disciplining yourself to go to the gym each morning, to bite your tongue instead of making a snide remark, to save instead of spending, and your mind sees all these as punishments, then you are working with conventional discipline. The consequence of doing something wrong. And because you feel you are punishing yourself with these acts, it makes difficult to always follow through with them.

A spirit of self-discipline, on the other hand, focuses on true and important desires. It is borne from the power of self and choice. The word "self" is intrinsic and powerful. Self-discipline follows the Law of the Seed: As you plant your seed in the soil, you keep watering it, providing nutrients of manure and sunlight, and staying patient all through until your seed germinates and bears fruit. Instead of focusing on immediate results or rushing out and digging up the seed for instant gratification. Instead of taking shortcuts, self-discipline preaches sticking to the strategies and systems that work. It preaches being conscious of your thoughts and actions and staying away from negative habits. It focuses on developing the "self" instead of destroying it.

Self-discipline is the locus of control inside you while conventional discipline is enforced by others where the locus of control is outside you. Self-discipline means you are not obligated to anyone and can make your own personal decisions and own choices.

Self-discipline is driven by the self and stems from within. It comes from having the freedom to make positive choices for yourself as you follow your inner teacher. A kind of discipline that works independently, offering lessons and growth instead of punishment.

CHAPTER 4

How To Develop Self-Discipline

Adding self-discipline into your relationships, worth ethic, nutrition and fitness is needed to be happy, lead a healthy lifestyle, and accomplish goals. Your choices should not be dictated by feelings and impulses. It should be informed and rational. Of course, you can train yourself to be self-disciplined. Through practice and repetition in your everyday life, you can create good habits, dissolve bad ones, and improve your decision-making process. This way, you live a life that free and full of healthy choices.

Self-discipline is not inborn. It is just like a muscle that toughens as you work out over time. Here are ways to improve your self-discipline.

1. Understand your motivation

First, before you can develop self-discipline, you should have a strong desire to accomplish a certain goal. A strong desire fuels self-discipline. Something needs to inspire that change. To stay focused on your path self-discipline, there must be a compelling reason why you are taking on a project or task.

What do you want? Why do you want it? Why precisely do you need to get it done? What desired outcome you have in mind? This could be a habit you want to develop or a goal you want to achieve. The more compelling your reasons, the stronger your self-discipline.

2. Eliminate temptations

Your self-discipline can be stronger when you follow the "out of sight, out of mind" principle. This means doing your possible best to remove all distractions and temptations from your immediate environment. Trying to adopt a healthy diet? Toss out the junk food in your fridge. Want to become more focused while studying? Switch off your smartphone!

3. Adopt a healthy and regular diet

Scientists have found that your resolve lessens whenever your blood sugar is low. When you are hungry, your ability to concentrate is impeded because your brain isn't working at its highest potential. Hunger not only reduces focus; it also drives pessimism and grouchiness. A poor diet can affect your self-control in all aspects of your life—from relationships to work. With healthy and regular meals, however, your blood sugar level is regulated and your concentration and decision-making skills are enhanced.

4. Do it even if doesn't feel "right"

To improve your self-discipline, you must be prepared to change your normal routine. This is often difficult and painful for many of us. The thing is, our habit behaviors are linked to the basal ganglia (a part of the brain responsible for memories, patterns, and emotions). However, our decisions are linked to a separate area of the brain called the prefrontal cortex. When a behavior turns into a habit, we go auto-pilot and stop using our decision-making skills. So, to break a bad habit and build a new one, you have to make active decisions; this process often feels wrong because the brain will fight the change and stick to what it has been programmed to perform. This is why you need to make active decisions even when you don't feel like it.

Procrastination plays a great role here. Self-discipline says: do it now! While a reprieve is good, embracing procrastination means sinking deeper into stagnation. Channel your energy into what matters the most and keep anchoring yourself to your goal.

5. Create an action plan

To achieve your goal, you need to create an effective action plan. This plan must come with mini-milestones and a reasonable deadline. Mini-milestones help you splitting your goal into manageable chunks—moving toward your goal in small pieces at a time. This way, you remain in control of the goal and you are not overwhelmed. By taking one step at a time, you simplify the process and begin to build momentum.

An overwhelmed mind easily procrastinates. And procrastination is a major stumbling block to self-discipline. Therefore, your action plan must have progressive steps and small wins as you edge toward your goal.

A deadline gives a sense of urgency and focus. Your path to self-discipline should have a practical deadline. A clear deadline disciplines your focus. When there is a specific end-date, your energy and resources are used properly in maintaining the needed momentum to follow through with your actions.

6. Have a self-disciplined mindset

Your state of mind is connected to your self-discipline. There are specific qualities—such as optimism, courage, enthusiasm, excitement, passion, diligence, passion, patience and diligence—you must imbibe. You must be committed to doing whatever is necessary to achieve your goal. You must be prepared to enjoy the process and make it a part of you.

Likewise, a self-disciplined mind knows the essence of priorities. A disciplined life is all about flow and structure. By focusing on the most important thing, you are less likely to get sidetracked with irrelevant things.

7. Visualize your desired outcomes

Being self-disciplined in one specific aspect of your life is the goal. Keep visualizing that desired outcome. This gives greater clarity about your goals and the actions needed to accomplish them. After you have defined your goals, imagine how you would feel when it comes to fruition. There is power in visualization and imagination. By creating a mental image of your target, you have taken the first step toward making it palpable.

Note that visualization is not the same as daydreaming. Visualization is built upon detailed and outlined goals. A daydreamer only fantasizes without lifting a finger toward any plan. When you visualize, remove all self-doubt. To be self-disciplined, you must learn to go head-on, leaving no space for negative thoughts to crawl into your subconscious.

8. Monitor your progress

Appreciate every progress you make toward your goal. Whether you are making use of a journal or calendar, track every progress and measure your growth. This will keep you focused and motivated as you reach your milestones. And even when you fail to reach a milestone, tracking your progress helps you see the adjustments you need to put in place to get back in the game and the pitfalls you have to eliminate. These pitfalls are often natural. The most important thing is learning from them and moving forward.

Find out the possible roadblocks and challenges that may pop up along the path to self-discipline. Take into account your weaknesses and commit time in sharpening the skills needed to overcome those lacking areas.

9. Be accountable and committed

You need an unwavering commitment to accomplish any goal. Long-term commitment powers self-discipline. But because there is often no accountable, we easily lose commitment.

Accountability is a focal point of self-discipline. For long-term commitment, you need someone to hold you accountable for your actions. A friend, family member, mentor or even a fitness trainer. Someone trustworthy checking in on you to assess your progress. This second motivating voice goes a long way in helping you achieve your goals.

You should also be accountable to your personal standards. Something to keep your straight when you go off track. As you find someone to hold you accountable, you must also hold yourself accountable for your everyday decisions and choices.

Also, look out for role models (family, friends, and colleagues) who have previously accomplished the goal you desire. From coaches to professors to even colleagues, many people are better and more experienced than you are. These are people who have gone through your current situation. Rather than stumbling about in the dark, toying with trials and errors, there is no harm in asking for help and direction. Using their experience and learning how they followed through with certain actions that got them these goals, you can work self-discipline into your personal journey. A supportive environment is important. New habits are easily formed when you have people to keep your committed, inspired and focused.

Commitment fuels self-discipline. No matter what challenges lies ahead, you must ready to stick to your goal. One thing I have found useful is to make a public commitment. For instance, I told several family members, friends, family members and colleagues about my plans to stop smoking. This way I was held more accountable for my actions and I was helped to stay disciplined along my non-smoking journey.

But commitment is never about your final goal. You have to be committed to each individual step that would lead to that goal. To avoid smoking, for instance, I did not just go cold turkey. I had to be committed to avoiding gatherings that would prompt to smoke, I had to attend Nicotine Anonymous meetings, use NRTs, and so on. Committing to little actions means being consistent with many habits that would culminate yours in the final goal. This way, you can avoid getting sidetracked sucked into the trap of instant gratification.

10. Be forgiving of yourself

Self-discipline is hard. There will be up and downs. The most important thing is to keep trying. Acknowledge your setback and move forward. Instead of lingering in frustration, anger, or guilt because you slipped back into a bad habit, forgive yourself and get back in the game. The longer you mourn your failure, the harder it becomes to get back on track.

That little voice inside your head, the one that always reminds you of the negatives, is capable of dragging you down to the gutters. Most times we are our own enemies on our path to self-discipline. We put ourselves down and think we will never be good enough.

Learn to forgive yourself. As simple as it sounds, forgiving oneself is one of the hardest things there is. But it's the most important. Understand that nobody is perfect. We all have our insecurities. But life needs not to be perfect for people to be happy about themselves. There is a virtue in acceptance, working to be better, and contentment.

11. Avoid the trap of perfectionism

Perfectionism is a self-sabotaging force. Perfectionism tricks us into thinking we are actually making progress. Perfectionism, in the real sense, is a defensive mechanism that shields us from doing the real work. To see perfect, we focus on the trivial tasks that give us some semblance of control Thereby, we keep fooling ourselves into thinking we are exercising self-discipline.

Expecting a lot from yourself is a good thing, but perfectionism can have a paralyzing effect if not properly handled—a roadblock toward your progress and achievements.

While, on the surface, being a perfectionist sounds nice: you have a keen eye for details, always looking to surpass expectations and focused on the next big thing. However, there are several ways in which perfectionism can serve a roadblock for you.

When you strive for perfectionism, you may end up procrastinating about the goals you are even passionate about. Because you spend a lot of time conjuring the perfect vision of how things should be done, you become overly detail-oriented and obsess about every issue. Soon, because it is painful expending too much energy on that project, you push it away and wait for that "perfect" moment—which may never come.

Another issue with perfectionists is the problem of skewed reality. Because by setting a high personal standard for perfection, they tend to expect more than what is realistic. Because they keep exhausting themselves physically and emotionally to achieve that "perfect" outcome, they end up missing the big picture due to their immense self-expectations.

There is a deep sadness that plagues most perfectionists. The desire for precision can create feelings of misery daily. Anxiety will always ensue when you keep obsessing over the outcome of a goal or when you keep beating yourself up about a slip-up. You eventually become dissatisfied and trapped, regretting even the smallest of things. In other words, perfectionists tend to keep battling depression, questioning their self-worth based on their output and performance.

When you are always striving for perfection, there is a chance that you are disregarding your health in the name of achieving the perfect result. To beat a deadline or adopt a habit, you practice self-neglect, allowing your health to fail over the years.

Finally, perfectionism can lead to compromised relationships. A perfectionist may put work above his or her loved ones and can be over-demanding of them as well. Perfectionists are also prone to lash out when things do not go their way. To overcome the roadblocks of perfectionism, consider focusing on what truly matters in your life, stop defining your self-worth by a list of accomplishments, and see errors as a chance to learn.

CHAPTER 5

The Principle Of Cause And Effect And How It Controls Everything You Do

The law of cause and effect (also known as "the iron law of the universe") plays a powerful role on your path to self-discipline. The law states that every effect has a precise and expectable cause. Every action or cause has a precise and expectable effect. For every effect in our lives, there is a specific cause.

This means that whatever you own in life is an effect brought about by a certain cause. In other words, to be become disciplined in a habit, you must be ready to take action (cause) and manifest that habit (effect) in your life.

The causes are the decisions you make and the actions you take every day. It does not matter if this decision seems trivial or unimportant, or major and important, every decision and action you have taken in your life is responsible for what you are currently experiencing in your life.

To find success in anything, the law claims, you must be prepared to perform specific actions. By being mindful of the things you do, and how they can push you to your goals, only then can you walk that path of self-discipline.

Life is all about making the right decisions and taking the right actions at the right time. You can become disciplined in your studies, diet, relationships, finance, and so on if you become mindful of those right actions and decisions. If you know what you want and know how to get there, then success can be yours.

First, examine the lives of the disciplined people (or people who are self-disciplined in the area you desire). Check out their actions, behavior, emotions, values, beliefs, habits and decisions to attract similar success into your life.

There are no accidents

There are no accidents in life because everything happens for a reason, the natural rule of cause and effect also states. This means that our universe is orderly. Like a game of chess, every move you make is a choice, and that choice is the cause, that cause comes with an effect.

Negativity gives birth to negativity. Violence gives birth to more violence. It is that simple. When you think positively and take the right positive action to complement your thought, chances are you will find yourself in a positive place.

Doing the same thing over and over again will get you the same result—the law of cause and effect establishes this. You cannot put in bad work and expect a good outcome.

Whenever I look back on my experiences in life, I could easily see the specific causes of my failure and success. The same thing goes for fitness and health, for contentment and misery.

For instance, I am fit right now because I have been going to the gym for a couple of months now. But if I halt my workout for two months, I will not be as healthy and fit and healthy.

Looking back on my past relationships, I can pinpoint at least two toxic relationships and how they had caused me misery. Therefore, going forward with any intimate relationship now, I would know the toxic traits to avoid in a person that might drive me to that same path of misery. The cause of my toxic relationships is my choice. And the effect is the toxicity.

The same things go for my work life. There certain things that have brought me to attain more of my potential. From communication to organization skills—things I had adopted from successful people. Likewise, there are also certain things that in my work life that would negatively affect my general happiness. Appreciating the law of cause and effect has taught me to make better choices as I strive to become more self-disciplined.

Be mindfulness of your choices

The law of cause and effect hinges on being aware of your choices. This means you have to see your emotional state, feelings, and thoughts for what they really are, and how they affect your life and decisions you make.

By being mindful of your choices, you can objectively take better control of your life and consequently make better choices.

Your thoughts are powerful: they can either make or destroy your life. Being mindful of positive thoughts is the easiest way to stay away from negativity. A positive frame of mind is a disciplined frame of mind. What you think is what you get. Every good thing you want to achieve in life is based on the kind of feelings, emotions, and thoughts you are mindful of.

While there are some things in life outside of your control, the law of cause and effects says you will often reap what you sow. Hard work will likely bring success than failure. Working out would likely bring fitness instead of obesity. If you embrace the darkness, darkness will continue to follow you. If you choose the light, your path will also be clear.

One of the best things I have ever done in my life is freeing myself from the hold of negative thoughts. Letting go of thoughts that would infect my space and feelings—thoughts that were driving me closer to more negative actions and more negative people, leaving me unhappy as I was unable to reach my full potential.

By freeing myself, I stopped making excuses and blaming others for my lack of discipline. I began to take full responsibility for my actions. Instead of remaining in a cycle of unease, frustration, and unhappiness, I applied the law of cause and effect and invested time in examining the choices that I have made and what I could have done better, and what positives I can take from the situation. In addition, I identified what actions I can take now to make my future a better one.

Give what you get

According to Sir Isaac Newton's Third Law of Motion, "For every action, there is an equal and opposite reaction." This a scientific explanation of the law of cause and effect.

The law of cause and effect has changed my life. Every one of my actions and inactions has brought me to where I am now. My poor health can be traced to my poor nutrition and diet. My mounting debt can be traced to my uncontrolled spending habits. Failure is not an accident. Success is not an accident. Every action I took (consciously or unconsciously) had consequences and produced specific results in my life.

In my personal relationships, the more honesty, compassion, love and respect (cause) I gave out, the more solid relationships – which lead to peace of mind, happiness, and fulfillment (effect).

If you want to be more disciplined in your life, identify the specific things you will need to do to become disciplined. Then take action! Making the first move to better is the hardest part; however, when you set things in motion, nothing can stop you. Then keep persevering. Rome was not built in a day. Success takes time. Success may not come immediately, but if you stay focused and continue to do the right things and fix where needs, you will eventually get the result you want.

CHAPTER 6

How To Manage Yourself

Self-discipline is possible when you can manage yourself effectively. Life is full of stress and hassles, which are often barriers to improvement. However, if you learn to manage yourself, you can overcome any challenge life throws your way.

Organization and time management

Organization and time management are major pillars of self-management. To become disciplined, you have to be organized as well as be ruthless with your time. Procrastination should be the enemy you avoid at every turn.

To effectively self-manage, make efficient use of your time: work smarter, not harder. Many people throw this mantra around a lot. Yet they end up getting overwhelmed, overcommitted and overworked.

So what does "working smarter" really mean? If you really want to work smarter, take a hard look at your daily tasks and start learning to prioritize them. Or, if necessary, just pass them off to others. If it can be done within 15 minutes, do it now. If it's going to take more time, schedule and prioritize it.

Working smarter means working with people smarter than you. No man is an island. Hire or seek the services of more skilled people than you are in certain areas.

Working smarter means controlling your habits. Each day, you have to be positive about your actions. A disciplined person is always in control, accountable, and a good time manager.

Working smart means taking things one at a time. Heavy multitasking doesn't necessarily translate to higher productivity. The fact is, you are much more productive if chart your day, figure out a to-do list, and prioritize your tasks.

Working smart means slowing down a bit. Feeling overwhelmed? Why not slow down and think about a better approach to the project? Just a few minutes of timeout can help see the effect of your actions.

Working smarter means working faster with fewer distractions. The internet, especially social media, is a time trap for even the most disciplined workers. Check yourself and monitor your addiction.

Working smarter means following up on your tasks. Of course, it sounds like a lot of work, but you'd be tightening up any loose ends that could cause problems down the road.

Working smarter means upholding teamwork. When positive minds work together and combine strengths, they work smarter.

Working smarter means valuing your time. If someone else can do that low-value task cheaper and better than you can pass it on to them. If every second of your work time not productively accountable, you're doing something wrong.

Working smarter means leveraging technology and automation. Thankfully, every industry or business has a tech platform. Save time for more important tasks by automating tedious ones. Remember to always be on the lookout for the latest tech

Finally, working smarter means having laid-out plans. You afford to be running in circles. An effective organization should be your watchword if you want more efficiency.

Set your priorities

Time is an asset that can be regulated. All it takes is for you to change the way you think, work and handle every day-to-day task competing for your attention.

Take a look at your most challenging undertaking for the day—the one that you're most likely to postpone, but also the one that will most likely have a great impact on your life.

A great rule of thumb is when in doubt, do the most important things first with utmost dedication and during your day's prime time—when your concentration and efficiency are at their peak. Don't be tempted to start your day with the easiest tasks hoping to reach higher outputs of productivity. If you want to be productive, tackle the seemingly most unpleasant and difficult task first. The trick here is that your body is still fresh and energetic for work. Moreover, nothing beats the satisfaction of knowing that you have cleared the biggest task of the day.

Additionally, never forget to plan your days. Write them down. Before you go about your business each morning, make out time to plan out your activities for the day. Planning for 10-15 minutes could end up saving hours of worry at the end of the day. Then assign your task to categories according to their order of importance.

<u>For instance</u>:

1.   **Must do**

2.   **Should do**

3.   **May do**

4.   **Delegate**

5.   **Delete**

After categorizing each responsibility, prioritize the tasks under each category also in the order of importance. Now, you can work from the top to the bottom and achieve better productivity. Break up a bigger task into smaller manageable ones. Psychologically, you will become more equipped to tackle the nest one.

Learn to know your limitations. It's often easy to see the major factors that keep you from accomplishing a task.

If you can identify this confining factor, you can directly eliminate it.

Success in both life and career is as a result of developing lasting habits. Learn to imbibe a habit where the main goal is tackled first every morning. These habits include setting priorities, conquering uncertainty and dealing with the most vital and tiresome assignment. Keep in mind that your habits are based on both physical and mental ability, so they can be learned and improved through repetition and practice until they become reflex responses.

Eliminate time wasters

Your dream is lost or won in your spare time. You need to dedicate time to achieve your life's purpose. Time is a scarce resource that most people take for granted. It's time for you to take it back.

Look at the lifestyle of winners. You will find them spending an unreasonable amount of time working toward the goals needed to achieve their dream. You won't find them arguing hours away on social media, barhopping around midnight on a Wednesday, or watching TV all day.

The fact is nothing worth achieving can be done quickly. While we all have the same number of hours in a day, what we do with our time differs.

For instance, what do you do when you get back from work? Between that late afternoon and before your bedtime, what type of time wasters steal your productivity? Do you become a couch potato or feed your social media addiction?

The antidote to time-wasting is the sacrifice. Start giving up on non-dream producing activities. Or at least reduce them to reasonable levels. Go to bed earlier. Don't constantly reply to social media messages. Time-block phone calls. Give up TV. Your time is just too precious for most of these time-wasters.

You have enough time to be successful. Every wasted minute adds up into hours that could have used to perform dream-producing activities.

Time wasters are everywhere and they can be humans also. Avoid people who always interrupt your productive hours with useless conversations. It's not about being antisocial; it's knowing what you want.

All you really have is time. Look beyond your nine-to-five and make the best of it. Instead of lazing off the weekend, why not start an online course, write a book, take up a vocation, or just follow your hobby.

Make a decision today to work on your 24 hours. Write a list of your weekly activities and identify the items that have no positive impact on your dreams—things that give you no fulfillment and joy. After creating this list, start timing each activity.

Of course, not everything you do has to gear toward your dream. Clearly, you have family, housework, etc. you need to engage in. The goal of this exercise is to discover things like TV, social media, small talk, etc. and either limit them or cut them out.

Make a conscious decision to make time your best friend by diverting it back into your dream.

Self-reflect

To manage yourself, you must quietly and honesty look at yourself. You must self-reflect: set aside time to assess your thoughts and feelings. Look in the mirror and describe what you see. The truth is that life is always trying to keep you in a "comfortable" routine. It is only when you reflect, you can review the effectiveness of your internal qualities and manage them. A minute or two of silent assessment can go a long way in giving you that much-needed kick- start to win at life. But remember that self-reflection isn't complete without self-awareness. True self-reflection comes with an awareness of your personality, your weaknesses and strengths, your beliefs and thoughts, your motivations and your emotions.

Create a personal heat map for self-reflection

The concept of a personal heat-mapping is simple: assign three different color codes to the most crucial aspects of your life.

1.   Green – all good

2.   Yellow – room for improvement

3.   Red – very bad

The whole point of a personal heat map is self-reflection and self-awareness. To manage yourself, you have to step back and assess where you are in life and where you want to go. It's like taking stock of every single area of your life, your distractions and goals.

A personal heat map lets you see the bigger picture with more objectivity. So you can come up with realistic plans to achieve your goals, improve the neglected areas of your life, and pursue things that bring fulfillment.

It's basically a status report for your soul. A visual tool you can use to break down those seemingly complicated aspects of your life into color codes. A list that not shows your strength and weaknesses but also provides a call-to-action on how to act on them.

Remember to make a long list of the important areas of your life. And while you are keeping everything listed and making room for me, you still have to keep it honest, though.

Take into account how you spend your time. Monitor your productivity, effectiveness, skills, education, health, finances, fitness level, character, relationships (with your significant other, friends and family), living conditions, creativity, energy level, career, spiritual life, etc. Assess your major life goals and how much fulfillment you're getting.

Understand your color codes and start evaluating yourself. If you cannot be totally truthful with your evaluation, ask a trusted family member or friend to help you.

Once you have figured out where you lie, you can then decide where you want to be. For instance, if the personal heat map shows that are overweight (your health status carrying a red color code), start making weight loss plans.

An action plan is your next step: Alter your current diet and start eating healthy, get a treadmill and do a 30-minute walk every sunrise. Drink more water. Get a gym membership. Consult a fitness professional, etc.

And as you are carrying out your action plan, keeping evaluating yourself with the personal heat map along the way. As you do this, you will be able to monitor your progress and make the necessary adjustments.

Finally, while you focus on improving the "reds" and "yellows" in your personal heat map, keep an eye on your "green."

CHAPTER 7
Making Friendship With Pain

Whether the pain we have experienced is mental or physical, tolerable or unimaginable, we all have all felt pain at some point in our lives. While it's maybe hard for you to see it now, pain is a natural and healthy part of the loss, hurt and grieving. You cannot avoid it. No matter how you try to bury the pain, it comes back harder.

One thing holds true in everything you do in life: the absence of pain is not the presence of fulfillment. Pain is important in your life. In fact, self-discipline comes from embracing pain and learning from it. To be in control of your life, you have to initiate a friendship with pain. You cannot know happiness without first knowing pain. You cannot know success without first knowing failure. Pain teaches you that happiness is possible, no matter the challenges of life. Pain is like a stepping-stone (a tool for growth).

Of course, it is never an easy thing to embrace pain; the process can be hard and dangerous. The good news is that facing your pain head-on delivers a deep dose of awareness when you need it the most. Awareness tells you what you really are and what you are meant to be, shedding off every lie you tell yourself. With awareness, you are then able to counter assumptions and limiting beliefs holding you back, as through pain, you can see your true purpose and nature.

Embracing pain also comes with exploring the depths of your life in an utterly different way. Your mind is filled with wounds of hurt and doubt, and only a deep cleaning and healing can bring you back to focus again. By embracing pain, you build a rebellious attitude against the negative fog and transform your life into your desired dream.

One of the surest ways to change your life is to confront your pain and become more aware of the choices you make and the consequences of those choices. Pain reminds you that your happiness is now. By acknowledging the hurt and not bottling it up, you become stronger. By facing it squarely, you free yourself of everything unhelpful and focus on the most important things.

Pain teaches the mind to be grateful. This is not to say that you want to remain stagnant; rather, it means you are mindful of your current state and are grateful to have what you have now. With this spirit of contentment, you gain a serenity that sees your place, person, situation, or thing as being precisely how it's should be at that point in time. By understanding pain, you free yourself from the victim mindset. Of course, you were hurt and injured, but you are not letting the pain reduce you.

Completely letting go of anger takes a good dose of commitment and discipline. Whenever we feel anger, pain, and stress, staying disciplined or happy is hard but necessary. But know that we cannot achieve happiness by just deciding to be happy. You cannot pressure yourself to be happy. You cannot just choose it. To find happiness, you must adopt a mindset that comes to terms with "not so happy" emotions. This involves allowing yourself to risk feeling the full length of human emotion—inadequacy, sadness, rejection, heartache, disappointment, connection, joy, contentment—and embracing even life's unpleasant emotions.

Only psychopaths and dead people don't feel painful emotions. Painful emotions are part of existing. Denying, dismissing, numbing or trying to distract yourself from feeling them wholly will create more pain and suffering.

If you truly want to experience pure moments of love, gratitude, connection, and joy, you must allow yourself to experience hurt, fear, sadness, and loneliness. By showing a "friendly curiosity" to less pleasant emotions and not downplaying or numbing them, you will be capable of constructively responding to the heartaches, hurdles and hardships life throws at you.

By being proactive with pain, you have some measure of control over the whole process. Instead of beating myself up for falling down, for instance, I became kinder to myself. Only then was I able to own up to my imperfections and acknowledge my mistakes; only then was I able to commit afresh to start again.

Lastly, understand that it is okay to feel unhappy. The fact is, sadness is the emotion that directs one to the pathway to happiness. If you have once experienced sadness and pain, you can be appreciative of what you have. And the more appreciative, the happier you will ultimately feel. Gratitude is a contagious emotion. The more you practice it, the more wholesome your life will become.

CHAPTER 8
Lifestyle And Nutrition

One of the most important things you can do is to be self-disciplined in your lifestyle and diet. When you are disciplined in those areas, your cognitive abilities are boosted. If you want to preserve your memory, enhance your mental performance and improve your physical health, start working out.

Exercise

Whether directly or indirectly, physical exercise can boost your physical health as well as your thinking and memory. It directly can lower insulin resistance, lower inflammation, and stimulate the release of growth factors—brain chemicals that improve the health, growth, and survival of brain cells, and the growth of new blood vessels in the brain. Exercise indirectly can enhance sleep and mood, and lower anxiety and stress.

Just like mental exercise, physical exercise also keeps your brain sharp. By sweating it out, you raise oxygen to your brain thereby reducing the risk of conditions that cause memory loss, like cardiovascular disease and diabetes. Exercise has also been shown to enhance neuroplasticity because it boosts growth factors and stimulates new neuronal connections. The more brainy you are, the more self-disciplined you can become.

Aerobic exercise is great for your brain and general wellbeing. Activities that keep your blood pumping and your heart healthy are beneficial to the brain. Regular aerobic exercise has been found to increase the size of the hippocampus, the brain area associated with learning and verbal memory.

Physical activities that involve complex motor skills or hand-eye coordination help can build your brain and self-control. Even the martial art tai chi—involving unhurried, focused movements, and the learning and memorization of new movement patterns and skills—has been reported to enhance cognitive function in seniors. Cognitive function is needed for verbal reasoning, problem-solving, attention, working memory, and planning.

If you start your mornings with light exercise, you can clear out morning blues and keep your brain active. This also protects your thinking skills and memory against the brain fog that comes with age. To overcome afternoon slumps and mental fatigue, a few jumping jacks or a short walk can reboot your brain.

How much exercise do you need?

Moderate-intensity physical activity, like brisk walking, is recommended at 150 minutes per week. You can start small until you get to your goal. Begin with a few minutes a day, and then raise the time by five or ten minutes weekly until you meet your target.

Asides walking, other moderate-intensity activities, like dancing, squash, tennis, stair climbing, or swimming, are great. Even household chores, like lawn raking or floor mopping, can keep your heart and brain health as well.

To keep you focused:

- **Find a friend to hold you accountable.**

- **Join a class.**

- **Monitor your progress, which motivates you to reach your goal.**

- **Hire a fitness instructor (if you can afford it).**

Studies believe that it takes about six months before you can reap the cognitive benefits of physical activities. Make exercise a habit, just like taking prescription medication. Patience is important while looking for the first results.

Diet

Your diet plays a great role in cognitive fitness. Research suggests food eaten is linked to memory capacity and self-discipline.

Diets high in fat and cholesterol (red meat, ice cream, cheese, butter, whole milk, etc.) might enhance the formation of beta-amyloid plaques (protein clusters) in the brain which are linked to Alzheimer's. As these plaques build up in brain blood vessels, they can harm brain tissue and deprive the brain of oxygen-rich blood needed for normal functioning, which can negatively affect memory and thinking.

However, heart-healthy diets rich in unsaturated fats are great for memory. Diets low in saturated fat lower the risk of obesity, diabetes, and high blood pressure—which can cause memory loss.

The Mediterranean diet, rich in healthy unsaturated fats (nuts, fish, and olive oil), whole grains and beans, cereals, vegetables, and fruits, has been reported to lower the risk of dementia. The Mediterranean diet can help enhance the health of blood vessels and reduce the likelihood of memory-harming stroke.

Omega-3 fatty acids

•   Fatty fish is a famous brain food. Rich in omega-3 fatty acids, fatty fish has been shown to reduce the level of beta-amyloid proteins in the brain. Examples of fatty fish include sardines, trout, and salmon.

•   People who eat fish often have been shown to have more gray matter in their brains. Gray matter houses most of the nerve cells that control emotion, memory, and decision-making.

•   About 60 percent of the brain is made of fat, and 50 percent of that fat is the omega-3 type. Your brain deploys omega-3s in building nerve and brain cells, so these fats are important for slowing down dementia and preventing Alzheimer's disease.

- When you don't get enough omega-3s, it can lead to depression.

- Non-fish sources of omega-3s include: soybeans, pumpkin seeds, broccoli, spinach, kidney and pinto beans, winter squash, flaxseed oil, ground flaxseed, walnuts, and seaweed.

Antioxidants and vitamins

- Colorful fruits and vegetables, as well as coffee and tea, have brain-boosting antioxidants. Omega-3 fatty acids.

- Coffee and green tea, rich in caffeine and antioxidants, can also boost your mental alertness, improve mood, sharpen concentration, and reduce neurological diseases, like Alzheimer's and Parkinson's.

- Blueberries and turmeric (active ingredient—curcumin), rich in anti-inflammatory and antioxidants, help fight against brain decline and neurodegenerative disease.

- Pumpkin seeds (rich in oxidants zinc, copper and iron) and broccoli (rich in vitamin K) have brain-boosting vitamins and antioxidants.

- Dark chocolate contains brain-boosting flavonoids and caffeine that improve mood and memory.

- Orange, strawberry, tomato, kiwi, guava and bell pepper (excellent sources of vitamin C) can help protect your brain against decline.

- Eggs (rich in choline and B vitamins) are great for correct brain functioning and mood.

- Moderate red wine consumption may also improve cognition and memory, and reduce the likelihood of Alzheimer's disease.

Stay motivated

You need the motivation to build a healthy and self-disciplined lifestyle. With food temptations constantly dangling around, you need a good deal of motivation to eat healthily.

Motivation works with the willingness to meet that desired goal, no matter what. It comes with learning how to deal with our different cravings, longtime comfort eating habit, and social situations. It means you are compelled to pay more attention to your nutrition and health in general. And when you put motivation at the forefront of your dietary goals, the magic is bound to happen in time.

<u>To stay motivated to live and eat healthily, follow these tips</u>:

1. Keep your goals small and measurable

While rushing things can get you overwhelmed, small and measurable goals seamlessly transition into your desired final goal. For example, instead of eating six servings of veggies and fruits daily, you can choose to introduce leafy green vegetables into your three meals daily, take (at least) 2 liters of water, etc.

We all want quick answers and results, but we can't just become healthy, strong or lean by just wishing. The truth is that, when it comes to living healthy, change is slower on the physical level than on the mental level.

But by making tiny changes, you're more likely to reach your bigger goal without burning out much quicker. Start by changing the small components—like swapping those processed items on our dish for a handful of greens—and never write off small winnings.

2. Make an exercise and food journal

Journals are very helpful in tracking your food intake. Many of us don't realize that every small bit adds up easily. A hand-written journal or a fitness app will come very handy here.

A journal also helps in tracking your progress, evaluating changes, and organizing healthy meal plans. Because you are monitoring your bites, you can look into your fridge and decisively clear out what isn't working. Keep a calendar too. Like a journal, a calendar comes with the physical assurance of your progress. Every meaningful goal must be time-bound. Mark that "X" on your calendar to see how far you have come and how much time you have left. Be diligent with your calendar and avoid procrastination. Remember that your goals have to be smart, measurable and realistic. Don't be tempted to rush things.

3. Focus on your plate

The dangers of junk food cannot be overstated. While fast foods may appeal to mouth and urgency, they are bad for your body.

Begin by adding nutritious whole foods to your groceries. Stack your fridge with more veggies, fruits, non-fat Greek yogurt, etc. Don't forget to experiment with new food and healthy recipes. Eating healthy doesn't have to be boring. Great, healthy recipes are scattered online and cookbooks.

Try out new things every day. Education and motivation work hand in hand. Surround yourself with the chance of eating a healthy diet. Educate yourself and avoid quack diet "hacks" floating around. Dedicate time to reading more about healthy eating: noting inspires more than real facts and real results.

4. Become more aware

Awareness comes into play, too, when eating healthy. Our body naturally resists change and urges us to quit. To overcome this, connect with your body and focus on your goals. Celebrate your success—not with a large slice of cake. Look for healthy meals that appeal to you and find total satisfaction in them.

Sometimes, overeating stems from our emotions. We unconsciously overeat to douse pain, connect to some childhood memories, etc. Avoiding a specific type of food can very hard in cases like this.

But with more awareness, you can begin to clear these barriers. Awareness says that the food you eat should nourish your body, mind, and soul—not the opposite. It says you are ready to confront your fears and failures and make that effort to eat healthily.

5. Use the support of family and friends

Don't beat yourself up when you slip up. Instead, get the help of people close to you. Someone who understands your goals and is willing to chime in when necessary.

Also, you can find a diet buddy and work together. Share recipes and pictures of healthy dished with each other. Meet up with them and talk about your progress and challenges. Encourage each other, give updates and ask for advice. This way, you are holding yourself accountable and mentally prepared.

Get online and find a support network, if you want. Alternatively, get a coach or take a class—just make sure you aren't doing this alone.

6. Create a vision board

Whenever you find that delicious recipe, take a picture and keep it. Make a collage of your most delicious healthy meals. If you can't make a scrapbook, get online and source for pictures of healthy meals you would like to make. Motivation is key. Visualize your success from dawn to dusk. Allow the excitement to build up and carry that energy to your kitchen.

7. Be prepared

Before you can eat healthy at all times, you have to be always prepared. To stay on track, store up a weekly plan of fresh fruits and veggies, smart carbs, good fats, and lean protein.

Always be prepared. For instance, you can make batches of quinoa or brown rice and roasted veggies at the start of the week and keep in the fridge—now you have quick and ready lunch whenever you are on the go. Remember to always bring along a healthy snack (bananas, apples, etc." when you leave home.

And if you eating in a restaurant, don't forget to check out the menu online in advance so that you won't get overwhelmed or tempted by unhealthy options.

Now it's time to clear your home of every "trigger" food: foods that tempt you to digress from your healthy path. And if they're for someone else, store them in the highest cabinet, somewhere easily out of reach for you.

Don't deprive yourself of good food all in the name of eating healthy. Just keep everything in moderation and enjoy the process. Don't be too hard on yourself when you slip up.

Puzzles and games

If you want to improve your mental exercise and recall information more effectively, do more mental exercises. Puzzles and other mind-stimulating games are a very interesting method of working on your brain muscle. Studies have shown that games that stimulate mental exercise enhance several aspects of your brain, including short-term memory. Short-term memory is needed to recall, remember and do quick mental arithmetic.

Since the brain never stops undergoing operational and structural changes, it stretches and gets tested (neuroplasticity), mostly due to mental exercises. So the richer your mental exercises, the better your brain becomes. As you learn more, do more and experience more, the greater the number of neural pathways that form in your brain. More neural pathways mean greater functional power for your brain. Your thought process and mental speed improve too.

In other words, mind-stimulating games enhance the growth of new nerve cells and reinforce the networks between them.

Because mind-stimulating games enhance neuroplasticity, you become faster and smarter when it comes to recalling short-term memory. If you exercise your brain via puzzles and brain-teasing games, your brain forms more neural pathways that help you take in and understand information with more ease and more speed.

Such games are reported to improve brain efficiency and elasticity because they provide challenging stimuli. Also, the skills acquired via mind-stimulating games can help you navigate problems and evaluate situations more effectively. You become more mindful of nuances and patterns faster. This helps you make correct decisions, access information, provide the right solutions, almost straightaway.

Jigsaw puzzles, for example, aid short-term memory as you recall colors and shapes and colors and imagine the bigger picture to determine which pieces will fit together.

Research suggests that brain-training games not only improve memory but also lower the risk of mild cognitive impairment and dementia. Even for older adults, these games can help keep their brains healthy.

Studies have shown that people who play mind-training games often have a larger volume of grey matter, which includes the cerebellum (associated with preserving motor control and body balance), dorsolateral prefrontal cortex (controls planning and decision-making), and hippocampus (associated with episodic and spatial memory).

Brain-stimulating games can help the hippocampus create a cognitive map, putting it to work. This may help lower gray matter atrophy that comes with old age.

As the mind is kept active through puzzles and other problem-solving games, the level of brain cell damage is reduced in Alzheimer's patients.

As these games help you make deeper connections, your mindset improves, your mood improves, and stress is relieved. This is because these games stimulate the production of dopamine in the brain. Asides reducing stress, dopamine—a neurotransmitter that controls feelings of optimism and mood—can help improve your motivation, concentration, and memory.

Sleep

You need sleep to function and be self-disciplined. Your brain is even working overtime while you are asleep. And there is a difference between the amount of sleep needed to keep you active and the amount needed for you to function optimally. To prevent the signs of sleep deprivation, you need between seven to nine hours of sleep nightly.

Studies suggest that a few hours more of sleep can significantly improve your critical thinking skills, problem-solving ability, creativity, and memory. This is because sleep is important to memory and learning.

According to research, quality sleep is essential for memory consolidation, because important memory-improving activity occurs during the deepest stages of sleep. Of course, you perform well when rested. Your brain is clear and alert. However, a sleep-deprived mind is always less productive and vulnerable to illnesses. Remember when you keep reading a sentence on a page repeatedly without getting it? With quality sleep, your focus is improved. A well-rested mind is more attentive and can absorb new information more easily.

A good night's sleep has also been reported to help the mind process and remember long-term memory. During sleep, your brain solidifies memories: connections between brain cells are strengthened and information is transferred from one brain section to another. People who remember every piece of information are most likely good sleepers. For example, while you are awake studying for a test or watching a movie, your mind takes snapshots of these events. During sleep, your brain reruns those events and forms new neuron connections to turn the experiences into long-term memories you can remember in weeks to come.

Researchers have discovered that the brain center that controls accuracy and speed is more active in people who get quality sleep after practicing a skill than those who don't sleep well. So whether you're looking to learn how to knit or play the piano, quality sleep can work wonders on your memories.

Scientists believe that during sleep, skills and memories are transferred to an efficient and permanent brain center, allowing for better proficiency the following day. Additionally, napping shortly after learning new information can improve retention. When you learn before going to sleep, information is stored better for the long-term.

Asides recalling old information, sleep can also help you create new concepts. During sleep, pieces of knowledge can be fused from diverse brain parts and experiences to create new ideas or "eureka" moments. This is helpful when you are trying to solve a problem.

Get started

- To get quality sleep, you need to have a fixed sleep schedule. This means going to bed at a fixed time nightly and getting up at a fixed time every morning. This means not breaking your routine even on weekends and holidays.

- Avoid screens (computer, phone, tablet, TV, etc.) an hour (at least) before bed. The blue emitted from these devices cause sleeplessness and reduce sleep-inducing hormones like melatonin.

- Reduce caffeine intake too. People react to caffeine in different ways. Some people are very sensitive—with morning coffee even interfering with nightly naps.

Note: The science of sleep is still very complex and studies are ongoing. There is still much to learn about the brain during sleep. However, one thing is established: your brain needs adequate sleep to make sense of your everyday experiences so that you can recall and function optimally every day.

CHAPTER 9

Why Failure Is The Key To Your Success

Failures and setbacks are not the end of the world, although they may severely drag you down for a while and it may be very difficult to get over them. The important thing is, learning how to properly deal with them sooner than later by "switching gears" and looking ahead toward new opportunities. While new opportunities are everywhere, however, you have to free your mind to be able to see them. After a while, you may even be able to laugh about your failures and setbacks, and importantly, they will become valuable "learned lessons."

Failures and setbacks are inevitable in life and career journeys. Your response can either lead to growth or disorganize you. While small setbacks can knock you off for a few minutes, more substantial ones can affect your entire life. So how do you handle roadblocks? How do you sail through that initial feeling of anger, disappointment, sadness or frustration? How do you self-reflect on your situation and obtain a better sense of self-awareness?

To become the best, you need to learn how to deal with adversity as well as move past it. Break down your failures into their basic components and try to work on each part positively. Remember that setback is an aspect of getting ahead. Take responsibility for the role you played in that failure.

Be introspective. Take time to process your current situation. Don't rush into action or jump into a hasty decision. Give your mind a break and clear it for a while. Find healthy hobbies that would refresh your mind. You can also practice reflection with mentors you trust. Apart from providing honest feedback and giving you a chance to vent, great mentors will also provide the encouragement and support needed to move forward.

By learning from failures and setbacks, you can plan ahead effectively. Then you will become capable of anticipating problems and coming up with contingency actions or plans. Look back into why you failed and make corrections. Was the setback as a result of insufficient resources, knowledge or manpower? Address that roadblock directly.

Don't let your failures trap you in a shell. Be open-minded and flexible enough to try out new approaches by looking at the issue from another angle. The fear of failure is deadly and even worse than failure itself. Take calculated risks and never insulate yourself. In addition, keep a positive attitude, no matter what.

Ultimately, understand that half the battle is won when you are able to keep a calm demeanor in the face of chaos. If failure and setbacks are properly leveraged, you become more confident in your judgment and abilities.

CHAPTER 10

Improving Focus And Concentration In Your Life

To improve your focus and concentration in life, be mindful. Mindfulness is a judgment-free, moment-by-moment awareness of sensations, feelings, and thoughts. It is a gentle acceptance of anything coming into your awareness without wanting to judge.

Mindfulness is capable of improving moods and focus and protecting you against depression and anxiety. By becoming mindful, you lower your stress levels, make your brain healthier, and make your body stronger. The more mindful you are, the more emotionally balanced and focused you become. You become more equipped to improve your self-awareness, decision-making and concentration. Mindfulness uncovers your own blind spots in terms of behavior, feeling, and patterns of thinking.

Because our minds tend to wander, mindfulness can be at first awkward to master. But remember that although reflecting on the past or planning for the future is crucial, the fact is that the only place we can actually be is here and now. The more you practice mindfulness, the more you can reap its benefits.

Be mindful of your breathing. Practice deep and slow breathing where your stomach moves as you breathe. Feel the sensations in your body. Acknowledge your thoughts and sensations and let them go. Pay attention to what is happening in your body. Notice what you smell, taste, hear, feel, and see.

Be mindful of your cravings. Notice how they settle within you. Addictions or cravings have a way of automatically pushing us to make quick moves to sate those needs. However, with mindfulness, you can acknowledge the conviction that the discomfort brought about this cravings will soon pass on by itself.

From doing the mundane like washing dishes to even taking a shower, you can effectively practice mindfulness as well. In these moments, it is easier to focus on your senses, thereby becoming calmer and reducing stress. A mindful walk down in the park can increase mental inspiration. To become a mindful walker, focus your attention on that genuine walking experience. Feel the ground beneath your feet. Without any distractions, put your senses to work—take in the feel, the smells, the sounds of the world as you walk through it.

You can also introduce mindfulness to your eating habits by engaging wholeheartedly with the eating experience and paying attention to the feelings that come up. Eliminate every distraction and be fully be present.

Life is full of running around. Mindfulness lets you step back, thus slowing the process down. It gives a sense of meaningfulness to everyday tasks. Note that there are no wrong or right answers with mindfulness: it's all about your awareness and the undiluted experience of living.

Practice more active listening

To grow yourself as an individual and become more focused, you need to learn how to ask the right questions and actively listen to people. Train yourself to become a good listener: one who listens carefully before responding rather than trying to dominate every conversion.

People listen for different reasons. We listen to learn, understand, obtain information or for enjoyment. But the fact remains that we never fully pay attention when others speak. From your co-workers at the office to your spouse at home, your mind is constantly trying to sift through every information coming in—and, ironically, may lose the crucial parts of the message in the process.

When you practice active listening, you become more effective at your job as well as improve the quality of your relationships with other people. Besides increasing your concentration, you improve your ability to negotiate, persuade and influence. By being a good communicator, an active listener drives success among people because he or she can avoid misunderstandings and conflicts

But you cannot become a good communicator without having a certain level of self-awareness. Always make a conscious effort to not only listen to the words uttered by another person but, more significantly, the complete message being passed along. This can only be done when you carefully pay attention and focus on what that person is saying.

To become an active listener, you must learn to overcome boredom or distractions when talking to another person as well as stop yourself from preparing a mental rebuttal while the other party is still talking.

If you have trouble keeping up with what someone is saying, consider repeating his or her words in your head as that person speaks. In doing this, you are mentally reinforcing that message and maintaining focus.

Although you may not necessarily agree with what the other person is saying, learn to acknowledge the message. An active listener is not a brick wall. Look directly at the speaker. Show that you are engaged in that conversion. Show that his or her message is getting across to you. Non-verbal communication, perhaps a simple nod, can show your undivided attention. An occasion recap of what has been said or a simple question shows that you are an active listener. Use your body language and other gesture to show your engagement while reading the speaker's body language as well. Use small verbal comments such as "uh-huh" or "yes" to encourage the speaker.

Whenever you are being spoken to, try to pay attention, show your undivided attention, provide feedback, suspend judgment and come up with an appropriate response. Remember that when you practice active listening, you can significantly develop better relationships and improve your focus.

CHAPTER 11

Meditation For Focus And Self-Discipline

If you are not focused or self-disciplined, try meditation. Real meditation is an antidote to anger, self-indulgence, and distractions. Meditation is a disciplined activity that many people struggle with. Your body does not want to sit still and meditate. Your body is more drawn to several meaningless indulgences. However, if you are prepared to meditate and breathe easy, you can make peace with your mind and access untapped strength.

Indulgence is giving in to anger, laziness, addiction or binge eating. It can also come from a place of beating yourself up for failing or not accomplishing a goal. Indulgence can mean being ungrateful.

Many of life's problems come from our lack of self-control. Fortunately, you can kick that habit by cultivating discipline through meditation. Meditation clears your mind of the dirt of indulgence and distraction—more like cleaning a dirty room. If you clean a room each day, you leave no room for dirt to settle.

However, when you leave a room unswept, even a clean one, dust settles and over time this dust becomes thick and disturbing. What daily meditation does is to sweep your mind and soul bit by bit each day, removing small amounts of dust before they become disruptive. Thereby solidifying your self-discipline.

Meditation puts yourself in the now. It focuses on the important things and pushes away unnecessary worries. A meditative mind is accepting of its situation. And through growth and stillness, such a mind is also committed to growth.

Stillness lets you find the truth. Just take a step back and breathe. Let your feelings come back and go. Take time each day to sweep the room that is your mind.

One of the most effective methods of self-discipline is through meditation. With meditation, you can improve concentration and self-awareness and find peace, which are core aspects of making beneficial decisions.

Peace is embedded deep inside us—deeper than our external distractions. Relax and keep calm and it would flow through every cell in your body. By meditating regularly, you can gain access to inner peace and find a real concentration. Meditation is capable of dissolving every wall of doubt, opening up and expanding space for growth in your heart. With daily meditation, you can find a way around your fears and tap into that inner serenity and joy that flow from the well of self-love.

Meditating works. Quick morning meditation will keep your mind ready and balanced for the day ahead. Meditation provides you that relaxing feeling capable of kick-starting your day for the better. It is all about ruminating about all you are thankful for while giving yourself some positive push.

CHAPTER 12

How To Develop Mental Toughness

Self-confidence is the secret to mental toughness. Confidence not only enhances your psychological wellbeing it also improves your professional and personal life. Self-confidence is all about taking action and not being a spectator in your own life. It is attractive and sexy—nobody can deny it. But confidence is a process. It cannot just pop up overnight. It is a habit that has to be cultivated time and time again. But confidence doesn't entail thinking that you are better than other people; it means not having to never compare yourself to anybody.

Confidence isn't something genetic; it can surely be learned. A child learning to walk, for example, must obviously take her first shaky steps. She will fall a hundred times, and shortly rise again, to run, dance and jump all over the place. The same thing goes for building confidence. You can falter along the way, but it will surely come.

You know you are self-confident when you start trusting your judgment, qualities, and abilities more. When you start believing in yourself and what you can do. Whether it is signing up for an art class or applying for a promotion, self-confidence is vital when you want to put yourself out there. Instead of wasting energy and time distressed that you are not good-looking enough, devote your energy to something you're good at.

You can't find confidence if you keep comparing yourself to others. The end result of this is often envy. And the more envious you become of other women, the worse you feel about yourself. This is some vicious cycle I have struggled to overcome. Comparing myself to people I thought were better than me eroded the little confidence I had in myself. I was killing myself with negative self-talk until I released that life is not a competition.

So I began to battle negative self-talk with positive affirmations. If your brain keeps telling you that you are not worthy of a date, a promotion or even looking good, remind yourself that these feelings are not necessarily true. Challenge negative self-talk by saying a few mistakes is never that bad. Positive affirmations helped in reprograming my mind to seeing myself in a better light. I was saying to myself: "Everyone likes me", "I am a great leader", "I am worthy", and so on. I wrote these mantras and repeated it to myself every morning. I kept it at my bedside where I could never miss it. And before I knew it, I was fueled each day to do great things.

Act the part of a confident person. It is all about faking it until you are making it. Even when you do not feel like it, act like it. If you want something so badly, act like you are deserving of it. Understand that this is not a feeling of entitlement but simply putting yourself out there. This has helped me many times in life. The more my mind keeps up a positive vibe, the more it keeps repeating it. Soon confidence will become more natural along the way.

I changed my dress sense as well. I began to dress smart. The smarter my outfits, the more people perceive me as important. I changed the way I speak as well. My voice became louder and direct. I was projecting my voice more confidently and getting noticed. I was no longer scared of sitting in the front row and putting myself in the spotlight. At events, I was no longer scared of being asked a question or pulled on stage. You must treat yourself accordingly: if you want to enjoy success, walk outside of your comfort zone and into the spotlight.

Your body language says a lot about you. Keep your body open. Try to walk tall in whatever you do. Keep your head up and look people in the eye when you speak to them. In keeping an open posture and not closing down or curling up, you show that you are both physically and emotionally sure of yourself.

Start leveraging your strength to build your confidence. Instead of being focused on your shortcomings or mistakes, embrace your strengths. Are you a talented businesswoman, a great cook, or an awesome public speaker? Focus on your strong points and you will easily see the value in yourself. Also, learn to fully accept compliments. No "buts." Never downplay your success or something nice said about it. Embrace it. There is too much negativity in this world so enjoy the goodness that comes your way—a free and easy way to believe more in yourself.

Low self-confidence can come from striving to be perfect. Perfectionists always set themselves up for disappointments. No one on the face of the earth is perfect. However, you can always do more, be faster, and better. I have stopped trying to do everything at once. I have stopped trying to be flawless. I just do my best, knowing that things do not have to be flawless to be good. I have learned to fight low self-esteem because I have stopped criticizing myself every time. Confident people are not perfect people—keep this in mind. Just be accepting and more tolerant of your shortcomings. Know that they do not lessen your strengths and talents.

I have learned to be appreciative of what I have already achieved. I realized that my self-confidence is strongly founded on how much I believe I am successful. As I noticed and became more self-aware of the successes in my life, my confidence skyrocketed. Know that you are an achiever, no matter what the world says about you. Instead of comparing yourself to the future version of yourself, look back and see how far you have come. Instead of comparing your present self to your dream self, look at what you have already achieved. Instead of feeling like a failure because your dream bod has not yet been realized, look back at the goals that you have already attained. See what you used to be a few years ago—see the progress.

Understand that everybody, even the greatest of people, has struggled with self-confidence issues at one point in time. Oftentimes, low confidence is a result of a bigger unaddressed issue—perhaps a traumatic situation from the past. It could also be a symptom of a mental health issue. However, if it is interfering with your education, social life or work, you have to seek professional help.

Self-love

Self-love is another powerful method of developing mental toughness. Self-love, the act of loving oneself, is an essential quality of inner strength. Self-love and selfishness or narcissism are completely different things. Love involves receiving and giving. The more you can give sympathy, attention, and care to yourself, the more you can bestow them on others as well.

It's an old spiritual truth: "We cannot love others if we don't love ourselves". Love blooms when it is shared, but love begins with "you." You are in charge of your deeds, choices, and most importantly, life. You have no right to neglect yourself.

Over the years, I have learned that loving myself is my first responsibility in life. It was only after I laid that foundation, my love for others came with strong perfection and clarity than I ever thought imaginable.

Naturally, when I'm in a tranquil state within, I relate to others in that same tranquil manner. But when I feel angry, insecure, frustrated, or scared, my relationship with others is clouded by a fog of blame and resentment. Only a mind at peace can know what love truly is. Sometimes, we get all stressed up because we feel responsible for other people's needs. And when those needs are unmet, our stress culminates into a feeling of failure and resentment.

Many at times, we are tempted to believe that others are more worthy of our love than ourselves. But withholding love from yourself means depriving others of it. Those times I found it hard to love myself, I consciously or subconsciously believed a part of me was unlovable.

A lack of self-love means we are a bit harder on our past actions than necessary. But sometimes, our memories of such past deeds tend to be exaggerated in their details and very subjective in nature. What you remember now of the most embarrassing moment that occurred years ago in school might be slightly skewered. Some nights we cringe in bed and throw regretful phrases like "I should have known" or "If only I had seen it then." But the truth is, there was no possible way of you knowing.

Loving yourself means accepting the fact that you're wiser than you once were. Self-love means knowing the only thing that matters is now. Granted, you were dumb back then. But realizing you were dumb back then shows you have grown since then. Remember, for you to come to terms with who you really are, never let who you might have been, what you could have done, or where you should have gone to hold your present state to ransom.

Self-love is difficult when you have someone always thinking less of you. But you should not let it bother you. Nobody is spotless. We are all trying to do our best to get by. The keyword here is "trying." As long as you are trying to better your present state, to be a better version of yourself, you do not need to worry about what the next guy is saying about the path you have chosen. Learn to appreciate yourself. Appreciate every little achievement you made and will make. Applaud every small shift toward the path of eating healthy and staying fit. And be proud of you and what you have become. Only then can you make real outward progress. Know that you are unique and you have a purpose in this world. The path you walk can be yours alone. Start embracing your individuality, then you can start seeing meaning in whatever you do.

Additionally, what you think of yourself is gold. Self-perception matters when building a healthy life. Be proud of the way you talk, walk, and look. Never underestimate yourself and fall prey to the grimy hands of self-loathing. But as much as we would like to think that we have control over our thoughts, we lose grip from time to time. Exercising control over self-loathing thoughts can get very hard, especially for someone who never feels good enough. Our mind is a funny thing. One moment you're having a grand day, come bedtime your head is running wild with self-loathing thoughts. Pain and misery are the outcomes of those thoughts. Start to look within yourself, checkmating the dangerous thoughts with positive ones. If we look at life from the surface point of view, the negatives always tend to overwhelm the positives.

Remember that nobody can really love you like you. When we are expectant of people to shower us with more love than we even give ourselves, we are setting up a relationship crammed with resentment. Nobody can love you like you. But when we realize this, it becomes too late. By then we hate those people who have "failed" us with their love.

It's your job to love you.

Be compassionate with yourself: a stern teacher can teach up to a point, but without a human side to him, no knowledge of sustainable growth can be impacted in his students.

I have accepted I have no control over how much my spouse loves me. I have accepted that I have no control over how much my children love me. I have accepted that I have no control over how much my friends love me. But only I can truly love me. Amazingly, whenever I feel like this, I am certain of the love that flows from everyone around me.

Self-love is self-acceptance. Learning to accept my good and bad side was no small feat. The hardship stemmed from the fear of remaining mediocre my entire life. When the world is moving so fast, sometimes we feel we are being left behind because of our defective traits. Everybody you know is getting married, getting a doctorate, buying a house – and there you are, feeling stagnant in your own small blessings.

Today, know that loving yourself doesn't translate to being satisfied with every part of you. It means you are accepting it for what it's worth. You accept that you can change what is changeable and also understand you can't mess with what is fixed. Yes, you can still improve your traits and still love yourself. The two never have to be mutually exclusive. Change isn't always going to be easy; in fact, it is often much harder to change than to keep things the same. However, the effort is well worth it. Even small changes, done consistently, can lead to big results.

When you accept yourself for who you are, you see your unique qualities and potential. You become more confident to face another day. You stop feeling the urge to copy others or compare yourself to them. There is power and inspiration when you come to terms with this. Your deepest fear isn't that you're inadequate. Your deepest fear is that you're powerful beyond measure.

CHAPTER 13

The Power Of Positive Thinking

There is power in thinking positively. Make a conscious decision to become an absolute optimist. Yes, life can get hard sometimes. Things might not always go your way. Everything seems grim and hopeless. The pressure is always intense. Even our planet is plagued with natural disasters, diseases, wars, and hate. But in everything, remember to be optimistic.

In fact, optimism is the key to success. One can never recover from failure without the right dose of optimism. Apart from improving the quality of life, optimism also works as the mother of creativity—you cannot come up with new ideas or create possibilities without it.

Optimism increases resilience. Whether you're an entrepreneur or a student, optimism has a major impact on your eventual success or failure. If you are ready to look beyond the present, you will become more resilient to face daily struggles. Of course, the road to success is paved with several bumps and dips, but it is your ability to pick yourself back up that makes all the difference.

While pessimism says wallow in your loss, optimism tells you to get back up, dust off yourself, and keep pursuing success.

Optimism fuels passion. It boosts spirits. Without passion, life becomes a drag. Cynicism, on the other hand, is a self-fulfilling prediction not likely to win you any success. You are not being naive when you believe in yourself. You are not being stupid when you spread optimism among others, as well. Just keep surrounding yourself with positivity. So to create a loop of positivity, keep befriending people who share your bright disposition and belief in a happier tomorrow.

Optimism isn't complete with setting your goals. You need to be focused on and mindful of your target. Put your goals and thoughts into writing and read it yourself every morning. A mindful heart knows that dark days will come and go. But if you can look to the future, instead of fixating on the past, success is yours. If you can learn from your mistakes, a brighter future is yours for taking.

Keep in mind that optimism alone isn't some magic potion. Always plan and execute as you look toward brighter days to come.

Working toward positive thinking

One of the greatest pathways to positive thinking is the act of love. And this pathway is only walkable when you have love within you. Your positive thinking is measured by how unconditionally loving and accepting you are toward others and, most importantly, yourself. One of Whitney Houston's songs says, "Learning to love yourself is the greatest love of all." To love others, you must love yourself too. Remember, you cannot give what you do not have.

Love comes from the choices we are making. Choosing love is to choose to be human. Every moment of your life, keep practicing it. Every second of your waking life, keep refining it and getting it right. It's all about the effort you put into it. Love is also the essence of being human. You can tell when it's there and when it is absent. Love embraces gentleness, selflessness, and vulnerability. And while it welcomes empathy, it also encourages toughness. Whether it's your doing or not, life is bound to be filled with tiresome chaos and drama. Finding peace and goodness amidst that rubble is a true recipe for positive thinking. One sign of positive thinking is that you have stopped contesting the nature of life.

Instead, you flow with it. You drop the pretense of believing that life should follow a certain pattern, a certain way. You start accepting life for what it truly is. You start to become more honest. Not only with others but also with yourself. Positive thinking births rewarding relationships. And a true relationship is founded on the pillar of honesty. Because another telltale sign of positive thinking is being bold to show your needs and wants. This requires standing tall in who you are, caring enough to be truthful, and fearless enough to bear the consequence.

Life will always have its fair share of pain; the more we resist pain, the more we fear it, creating more pain and suffering. Despite the pain life has to offer, positive thinking offers unconditional love to self as a gift. When you start greeting pain with calm curiosity, you can tell you're on the path of finding positive thinking.

Positive thinking destroys self-loathing

Positive thinking is the secret to many of life's problems. But thanks to the lure of self-loathing, we never fully utilize the power of positive thinking. The thing is, self-loathing and shame go hand in hand. We tend to battle with anxiousness and depression. We mold all the self-torture and stress – and they became part of our lives.

It's time to start looking at the person in the mirror. Even beyond him or her. Many of us are shy of the mirror, but we can't all be supermodels on the cover of fashion magazines. The media and pop culture have brainwashed us over the years with their own idea of beauty. We want that that unblemished skin, pearly white teeth, and a skinny beach bod. Of course, having all these qualities will make you a sight for sore eyes, but does beauty really end there?

Take a look in the mirror and see. There's beauty in those eyes, freckle, nose. There's a peculiar deep within – untouched by wear and tear of body age or physical altercation. When next you hate yourself, search for that one quality in you are proud of. We all have our imperfections and weaknesses and imperfections, but we shouldn't let them dictate our lives. For some time, I never felt the compliments directed to me, no matter how genuine and heartfelt were never justified because of my weight.

Sometimes, when all our doubts, fears and insecurities wrap ourselves up, we always come up with the idea of

"I wish I was somebody else." More often than not, we think and believe that someone or rather most people are better than we are—when in reality, the fact is, most people are more scared than we are.

You spot a totally eye-catching girl sitting by herself at a party, casually sipping on a glass of wine. You think to yourself, "She looks so perfectly calm and confident." But if you could read through her transparent mind, you would see a bunch of clouds of thoughts and you might just be amazed that she's thinking "Are people talking about why I am seated here alone? Why don't guys find me attractive? I don't like my ankles; they look too skinny... I wish I was as intelligent as my best friend."

Isn't it funny? We look at other people, envy them for looking so outrageously perfect and wish we could trade places with them, while they look at us and think of the same thing. We are insecure about other people who are insecure about us. We suffer from low self-esteem, lack of self-confidence and lose hope in self-improvement because we are enveloped in quiet desperation.

Stop thinking of yourself as a second-rate being. Forget the repetitive thought of "If only I was better looking... if only I was thinner." Accepting your true self is the first step to self-improvement. We need to stop comparing ourselves to others only to find out at the end that we've gotten more reasons to envy them.

You may not even realize how much you listen to negative self-tapes. A lot of times these are happening below the conscious level. We're prone to criticizing ourselves harshly. We're too caught up with self-loathing that we fail to step back and see the good of our existence. We fail to acknowledge that our lives are worth something. Here, the power of self-talk is massive. You are your number one supporter. Your opinions and thoughts about yourself are your strengths.

Positive thinking builds self-esteem

Your self-esteem is a result of the feedback from people around you and how you interpret it. Choose what you listen to; it can either reinforce your self-confidence or destroy it.

Failure and criticism cause pain. We can try to hide the pain, subdue it and push it aside, but the pain never leaves; it continues to undermine our sense of security. Unconsciously or consciously, we would agree with the negative comments and accept them as part of who we are. Because of this, it becomes hard to see the world in a positive way. The longer we dwell in our pain, the more paralyzed and helpless we would feel whenever it comes to making positive changes in behavior and thoughts.

Finding the motivation to change is a process. Moving away from negative thinking doesn't happen instantaneously. Remember that you're fighting against a mass of bad experiences and deeply embedded beliefs.

Positive affirmations have helped me times without number. Affirmations, subconsciously and consciously, feed our minds because, in time, those repetitions turn into our deep truth. Always be approving of yourself with your words. Say aloud when alone: "I have the right to feel good about myself" as many times as you can to program it into your mind. It's vital hearing yourself utter these words aloud. I found out that the more positive feedback I received and internalized, the more secure in myself I felt. The more negative the feedback, the more insecure I felt. Of course, you cannot control what others say about you. But you can choose how you react to them.

CHAPTER 14

Why Negative Emotions Can Fuel Your Success

It is easy to lose hope in yourself and fall into a deep depression. Of course, some past issues in our lives that hinder us from moving forward. This could be emotional challenges or past trauma. Events, beliefs, and emotions are often interconnected. Some underlying issues triggering and driving us to emotional wrecks. This could stem from your past emotional baggage and unresolved emotional conflicts. Childhood issues of abandonment and neglect, for instance, could trigger overeating.

We tend to shy away from such matters. Still, you can't feel strong without first examining your weakness. In facing weakness, you learn how much there is in you, and you find a plan for real strength. We don't identify the impact events have had on us until years later when we start unscrambling those buried, unhappy moments of our lives. When you confront that weakness, you're breaking down internal barriers and clearing the damaging baggage of past events that continue to affect your life. Allow yourself to say aloud your feelings. Say what you want to say. Healing is possible when you're ready to have a new compassion for yourself.

Healing is crucial in building inner strength. Healing means forming a new relationship with yourself and becoming more aware of your own stress and the anger and sadness you have long been holding inside. We believe the hurtful words we're told even before people say them to us. Oftentimes, we don't have the appropriate response of healthy anger so we tolerate such obscenely unnecessary attacks. We let those words tear us down because we feel they are true. We feel powerless to express our anger and even hurt ourselves more. We spend years obsessing over our errors, turning it into a barrier standing between us and our future.

On the journey to true mental strength, be ready to meet your own needs and desires by standing up for yourself. Clearing the emotional impact of hurtful words is possible. The key here is letting go of the negativity. Releasing the wound and the shame doesn't mean burying your anger. On the other hand, don't be quick to force yourself to forgive and be in denial of how much the words hurt. It's okay to be angry. It's okay to take your time before moving to a place of compassion for the people who have hurt us. It's vital to take your power back in a warm and loving way with forgiveness. But take your time to get there.

Then look inward and identify all those limiting beliefs that are restricting progress in your life. Your belief is a thought you have repeatedly. Your beliefs impact your confidence. Your beliefs can support you or limit you in the journey toward mental toughness.

Your experiences are reflections of your beliefs. Believing that I wasn't good enough (or that I wasn't strong or smart, or attractive enough) was like giving myself a life sentence; it left no room for any other possibility. Holding this belief, I unconsciously looked for evidence to support that belief and took action (or refrained from action) that supported it. I was projecting my insecurities on others and interpreting events in ways that support the belief even when it was causing me pain. And I was unconsciously seeking out or trying to be with people who confirmed my belief. I even played down and rejected positive compliments and only focused on the negatives people tell me.

When we feel we aren't worthy, we find ourselves gravitating toward folks who mirror that belief back to us. But when we stop believing in those negatives about ourselves, however, we won't be able to tolerate these disrespectful people anymore. Believing we deserve support and love is the foundation of self-love. With self-love, you then create a supportive community of people capable of loving and supporting us. Note that getting here is an overnight thing.

Question negative beliefs

When you hold on to negative beliefs, the world seems threatening and scary. You can escape that world and prevail. Negative beliefs, whether gotten from our environment or inherited from our parents, often appear disguised as facts. The most important thing is to never stop questioning your negative beliefs. Despite the deep-rooted resistance you feel letting them go. By questioning, you weaken emotional strongholds holding you back. Why should you feel less worthy because of your size? Why should you feel like you've grabbed the shortest straw in the gene pool with your "bad genes"? Take a step back and ask yourself, is this actually true? This is the first step to accepting empowering beliefs.

Next, identify your limiting beliefs. These negative body beliefs are controlling. They make you sit on the sidelines, reluctant to partake in your own life, refusing to do things you enjoy doing. What negative feedback have you been replaying from others to support your limiting beliefs? When did you learn that you aren't (smart, good, pretty) enough? What events have you used as proof to back up your negative beliefs?

By identifying limiting beliefs spread across different areas of your life—which have over time solidified themselves into one big story you're telling yourself about who you are and what's possible for you. Once you're addressing the limiting beliefs that have shaped your story, you can create a new story and make incredible, natural progress. This starts when you stop obsessing about your negative emotions and start obsessing about self-love.

CHAPTER 15

How Zen Philosophy Can Help You Achieve Your Goals

Do you set up goals and end up not accomplishing them? Make exciting and grand plans to be better and later slip back to your old routines and habits?

Thankfully, you can find a solution to this problem with Zen philosophy and the teachings of Buddhism. But Zen philosophy focuses on living in the moment—how can we use this to achieve our goals?

The fact is goals often come with deadlines, and deadlines are important in pointing out the path to that future goal. We shift our focus to the future often when setting goals. We remove ourselves from the "now" and focus on what is to come. This way, we invite in anxiety on our path to that goal. With anxiety comes a loss of motivation and crumbled dreams.

Zen philosophy says before you set any goal, you must know what your core values are. You must be mindful of who you are. Your values must connect with your goals for your goals to be achieved. Do you value success, adventure, love, passion or security? Only you can determine your value.

Instead of staying fixated on your goal, focus more on your values. Your values are why you want those goals. How will those goals will make you feel when you accomplish them?

Additionally, leverage the power of visualization to see yourself accomplishing that goal. Bring your goal to the present. Zen philosophy teaches the power of mindfulness and visualization so well. Spend time each day to think about what you want your future to look like and your values. Imagine yourself in a state of living those values. Think about what you want your day would look like.

Then slow down and be mindful of what is happening around you. Do this without judgment. Instead of being aggressive with yourself or getting frustrated when things don't go your way, appreciate where and what you are right now. Instead of focusing on what you don't have, visualize the future you want and stay in the moment like that future is already yours. Stay in the present moment and remain grateful. Then your goals will come through because you have mentally prepared yourself to be successful.

CHAPTER 16

Forming Good Habits And Breaking Bad Ones

To form good habits and break bad ones, you must start seeing change as an opportunity. For most of us, we are stuck to our bad habits and comfortable with it. We fear change. So we become reluctant to embrace it because it threatens our present comfort.

Remember that change is a normal part of growth. Adjusting or adapting to it should be your priority if you want to break free from that bad habit.

Still, change is the only constant thing in life. When you embrace it, you give room for hope during unexpected or challenging life events. Change is an opportunity to do something different or even better.

Create rituals

To form a new habit, you have to make it a ritual. Rituals can be manifold, from lighting up a candle out of gratitude or grief to doing someone special with your loved ones on specific days every year. It could be something as mundane as showering or taking coffee to willful commitments like exercising or reading a book before bedtime.

Rituals increase the consciousness of the moment; in families, they solidify bonds and thoughtfulness and serve as landmarks throughout the year.

Rituals are vital to achieving happiness. Even day-to-day life is filled with personal rituals: behaviors that are structured, predictable and established. Behaviors that bring orderliness and flow to life, giving you a sense of purpose and direction. And by reminding you what is crucial at the moment, they provide a sense of continuity, focus, and stability.

From business to social to personal, we are all ingrained with rituals. They affect your social health and personal health. They determine who you truly are and form your habits—habits that shape your life experience, whether positively or negatively. Whether you succeed or fail depends on your rituals—as they can likewise build new structures and values.

Success needs a great deal of self-control and willpower. However, the human brain is only capable of a limited amount of them. Often when you exert your mind's willpower or self-control, it negatively affects your creativity and ability to focus. But with ingrained rituals, specific aspects of your behavior becomes routine, therefore you never have to push yourself to perform certain positive actions to get positive habits.

Contrary to popular belief, rituals, especially positive ones, are not time-consuming. Having a ritual is all about paying attention—one important skill needed to survive on both a personal and career level. Starting from when you get up in the morning to when you go back to bed, positive rituals lead to a better quality of life. Be on a lookout for rituals that brings joy, energy, and gratitude to your life. Rituals help you feel more connected to your loved ones. Rituals that make you feel more productive.

Whether it's sorting out your worktable, celebrating your son's birthday or enjoying a religious festival, rituals comprise of productivity, gratitude, and devotion. With them, you can form and sustain habits. Communal rituals move and motivate us, building communities and families. They help in marking significant life events while giving you an avenue to express our sorrow and joy. Personal rituals, on the other hand, are customized to your needs, providing inner peace, building bonds and improving mindsets. Pick up a ritual today.

Let your 'idle' time work for you

During your day, you get plenty of "idle" time. This includes the time you spend waiting for something, cradling your toddler to sleep, having your bath, or watching a game on TV. However, by leveraging this time, you can manifest a new habit easily.

Obviously, you are calmer during your idle time. During those calm portion of your day, you can invest in new hobbies. Having consciously stepped away from the hassle of the day, you now

Making the best of your commute time

Commuting does not have to be lost time, in contrast, it can be a great opportunity to further educate yourself regularly. You can read (on public transport), listen to audiobooks, language trainers, and so on.

Successful people start their day with the end in mind— they understand what they wish to achieve. Instead of checking social media or your emails on your way to work, ask yourself what you can do now that you'd have trouble making time for elsewhere. Why not start

Why not use that time to exercise? If you could walk or take a bike to work, please do so. A 15-minute stroll every day can make for a healthy heart and weight. Staying healthy while commuting is like killing two birds with one stone. Apart from staying fits and healthy, you will become more productive at work. And even when you are bus or rail rider, start getting off early a few stops an extra 10-minute walk.

Why not network and socialize? Don't just carpool because you want to save on tolls and gas. The mood-boosting effects of driving to work with friends and colleagues can skyrocket your work productivity, as you discuss work projects and network,

Why not get smarter? Successful commuters are always enriching themselves mentally. Learn a new language, read the whole Lord of the Rings series, or just study a course. Find inspiration and better yourself on your way to work. Those minutes on the train add up, you know?

Why not make the best of your "idle" time? While commuting, you can also use that few minutes of solitude on the bus to see the big picture of your life. What plans are you taking to accomplish your goals? How are you going to negotiate that raise or deal?

Get feedback

Feedback describes helpful criticism or information about prior behavior or action from one person, given to another person (or group) who then deploys that information to improve or adjust present and future behavior and actions. From performance exhibited to performance expected, information is exchanged.

When it comes to personal development, requesting feedback is still much of an untapped resource, at least on the private side of life. Requesting feedback from people you trust and people who know you well can catapult you toward your better self. Honest, constructive and specific feedback is something very special and, in return, you can offer the same to the respective feedback provider.

Constructive criticism can show you the error of your ways while allowing you to make amends and continue learning. Continuously ask for feedback. Both positive and negative feed can be helpful in life, career, and academics. Don't just expect feedback. Deliberately request it. This is a great way to highlight your strengths as well as weaknesses. When it comes to effective feedback, everybody wins, both the receiver and the giver.

Feedback is always everywhere you look. Whether it's your professor, boss or even friends and family members, trusted feedback properly communicated can improve the quality of life. Feedback can motivate you to perform better and build better (professional or personal) relationships.

When approaching anyone for feedback, make helpfulness your priority. The giver should feel at ease to give you honest feedback without the fear of hurting your feelings. Provide the giver adequate information concerning the situation and keep your interaction conversational.

Hearing feedback on past errors is good, but endeavor to ask what you can do to avoid them in the future. This shows that you are not dwelling on the past but focused on moving on.

Remember to tailor your questions. Keep it short and simple. Also, take notes—stopping to take notes shows that you value the other person's contribution. No matter what, avoid being defensive. Even when you are told something you don't like, reduce the urge to begin a debate. Instead of reacting defensively, be thankful for the feedback. Appreciate the other person's time and effort.

CHAPTER 17

Daily Habits And Exercises To Beat Procrastination And Achieve Your Goals

Procrastination is a killer of dreams and self-discipline. Life is getting increasingly fast and complex. We cannot afford to be stagnant on the path to our dreams. Without adopting certain habits and exercises, you cannot find success.

Start early

One of the best ways to overcome procrastination and achieve your goals is by starting your day early. Science agrees that early birds, people who constantly beat the morning rush, have better mental strength, more optimism, and greater energy levels than their night owl counterparts.

Ever wondered what would happen if you wake up 2 hours earlier than usual each day? That's 730 hours a year. About 30.4 days in a year. That means you get one extra month to be active than most people in a year. Being the early bird is not magical. It's a skill you can learn and adapt to a habit. Imagine already being 2-3 hours ahead of your colleagues before they arrive at the office. You are fresher, with fewer distractions, and better equipped to focus on the high-priority tasks of the day.

For most of us always wallowing in the drowsy lethargy of mornings, productive morning people seem like enigmas to us. Are they biologically engineered or just amped up on caffeinated willpower?

The truth is, your energy level is highest in the morning. Like an energy bar, it slowly declines as the hours go by. First, you need to get adequate sleep the day before. If you aren't getting enough quality sleep, your morning (and even entire day) will be laced with excessive grogginess. No matter your level of discipline, you cannot successfully begin a habit of productive mornings with poor sleep. You can't cheat nature. It will fight back. You need to start sleeping early. Allow your body to adjust to the initial fatigue. Of course, you may start slow, but once you begin, you can build up momentum.

Apart from the duration, the quality of your sleep is likewise important. Begin by creating a more relaxing evening routine. To get quality sleep, you need to set a routine that slowly shuts off your body before bedtime. For example, you can shower, read a book, listen to relaxing music, drink warm milk, etc. Remember to avoid caffeinated drinks and heavy food before you go to bed.

Flush out the fear of missing out on all that delightful evening fun. Although a wild nightlife is exciting, remember that it's probably incompatible with a productive early morning habit. Dim the bedroom light, turn off the TV and computer, and put the cell phone on mute.

Then you need to plan your mornings the night before. Clear every mentally draining and time- consuming action before you go to bed. From preparing your breakfast to packing your lunch to choosing the clothes to wear, save mental and physical by doing them the evening before?

It's crucial you have a clear plan for doing work that matters. With a clear plan decided the evening before, you can beat every early-morning distraction and uncertainty. Getting up early is easy when you love your job or when you are passionate about a goal. Have a reason to wake up each day, find your passion, and you will never be short of enthusiasm to hop out of bed early before sunrise.

And once you're awake, kick-start your day with a light but nutritious breakfast. Don't forget to do some light exercise early in the morning. Science says we release endorphins (feel-good stuff) when we workout. In fact, as your muscles stretch, it takes in more oxygen, thus keeping your tissues refreshed.

Make a "to-do list"

Between work, school, social hangouts, workout, and other real-life obligations, meeting our goals and making deadlines is never easy. This where an efficient to-do list comes in. A to-do list is a classic component of being productive. While pen and paper might appeal to the traditionalist, neatly designed to-do list apps can become your invaluable and ever-patient personal assistant.

When creating your list, keep it simple and realistic. If you're running on a 24-hour timeframe, work within your limits. Begin with the most important tasks. Preparing a to-do list is not only about ticking off items; you need to continually re-prioritize these items by rearranging their order of importance on your list. After acting on your action plans, always re-work your list to keep other untouched priorities at the forefront.

A to-do list also gives room for you to jot down every action item that comes to your mind during the day. So even when your memory fails, a to-do list saves the day.

Know that it's not a crime to start easy. Whether you're doing the dishes or folding your laundry, a few crossed-off simple tasks before the important ones can give a feeling of accomplishment and productivity.

Most importantly, avoid writing down action plans that sound too vague or daunting. You need to remove that fear factor by breaking down goals into manageable smaller tasks. So instead of writing "I will work on my book," try something more specific, like "write the first half of chapter five" on Tuesday and "write the second half of chapter three" on Wednesday.

Additionally, time is of the essence. A realistic goal is time-bound. Place a time estimate next to items on your list. And if you want to stay accountable to your list, introduce a trusted second party to watch over you. Post it on the refrigerator or share it on a synchronized to-do list app— nothing beats the morale of teamwork.

Finally, remember to be flexible. Give yourself some cushion time to get things under control.

Take it step-by-step

Procrastination occurs when the task seems too big. Break big tasks down into manageable steps. When the project seems too daunting, the complexities can weigh you down. You look for motivation and it never comes. You put off the big task and prefer to do something else. The fact is, the way a task presents itself to you has a major effect on your level of motivation to take action.

Rather than being overwhelmed by big goals (and thus never attempt to achieve them), break them down into manageable steps. This will make the project less stressful than you had originally anticipated.

When faced with a big task that seems overwhelming, break the task down into smaller manageable steps. Doing this will assist you in eliminating procrastination and stress. So once you actually begin, your impression of the project will change for the better.

Now, how do you break down large projects? Splitting a large project into small achievable parts is no small job itself. You have to work with your imagination and create a functioning methodology.

First, have a solid idea of the big picture. Then create a realistic plan to help you stay on track. Know what your end goal is meant to look like. Then do a step-by-step assessment of each part of the project by building a mind map. As mentioned earlier, a mind map helps you split the main subject into several branches. Each branch describes each task you need to achieve to make your overall objective successful. And if a smaller task seems unachievable, break it down again as you spread out your branch.

Form a timeline. Start thinking about the most reasonable order of carrying out each part. Now you have to start arranging every listed/smaller task in chronological order as they lead to your final goal. Next, implement a deadline for carrying out each task.

The next stage is setting measurable milestones as you complete the smaller aspects of your major goal. This act alone fuels your motivation as you cross off smaller tangible goals. In the end, make up some time to review your final project.

Ultimately, fight the urge to put off tasks that seem insurmountable. It's no surprise that procrastinators, after waiting until the last minute, are the most stressed group of individuals. Understand that any project would become less daunting and more manageable when you set priorities and break it into smaller tasks.

Continuity & endurance

Continuity and endurance (alongside discipline) are some other important factors to achieve your goals in life. They are also the essence of a successful life or career. These two factors separate winners and losers. Continuity means you're willing to keep the fire burning for a long time, never losing momentum, no matter what. While endurance means you're ready to withstand any challenge for a long time.

These two concepts share a similarity: time and discipline. Once you have both locked down, you can deal with the consequences of your personal decisions and stick it out to the end.

Many fail in life because they lack the endurance to keep pushing on. Many settle for less because they lack the continuity to keep pushing on. Most people overestimate what they can achieve in a month but underestimate what they can achieve in a year. They lack the foresight to continue and endure.

The road to success is littered with roadblocks, but only those who keep their end goal in mind can scale through every difficulty. And as time and experience come to play, they set a nice pace for themselves, and become unstoppable.

It takes time to achieve mastery. It takes time to achieve success. You can't afford to quit because you are bored or tired. You can't just stop improving because you aren't improving fast enough, or because you think you have done enough to move on to the next thing.

The good news is, with a little bit of discipline, endurance and continuity can be learned. You can build endurance when you start rejecting every temptation urging you to give up. You can build continuity when you remain focused in spite of unexpected circumstances.

Of course, it is easy to get to a point where you feel you can't or shouldn't continue on. It's easy to throw in the towel and settle for a meager paycheck when you know your qualifications can get you something better. It's easy to abandon that innovative startup because you didn't make a bank at the end of the first year.

But life doesn't always play out like that. The truth is that you aren't your best self when you feel you are at the top of your game. It's actually when you are plowing your way through your bleakest hours that your real strength shows. If life throws a blow, take it like a champ, and dust yourself up. Continue and endure—and while you celebrate today's victories, always keep your eyes on the big picture at the end of it all.

CHAPTER 18

How To Create A Daily Plan To Build Your Success

Success comes with being honest with yourself and dropping all excuses. Most times we lie to others for some reason or the other. In a few of those cases, that lie would seem like the best choice in a sea of bad options. But to lie to yourself, though? That is the worst of all. It happens every time more than you care to acknowledge. You convince yourself that you are doing the right thing, that you made a wise financial choice, or that everything is fine. When reality proves otherwise, you stick to your guns and refuse to back down.

As human beings, we always want to be in the right. We want our actions, beliefs, and attitude to line up together. A rift in these things would make us feel uncomfortable, so we are very quick to justify our actions, right or wrong. But there is a price to pay for always wanting to be right: you lose plenty of opportunities to grow, to improve on your outlook of life.

Another reason we lie to ourselves is that we fear getting hurt. We don't want to rock the boat, so we make excuses. We turn a blind eye to obvious wrongdoings and say it can't be as bad as it looks.

We also lie to ourselves because we dread change. We are scared of leaving our current space, no matter how toxic it gets, because we are held down by the power of denial. We keep holding to false beliefs that clog up space for new opportunities, ideas, or people.

Stuck in a bad relationship or a terrible job? We choose to wallow in denial or make excuses for the lie. A lie that things would get better on their own. A lie that you can never do better than this. A lie that you have invested too much time and energy in your ignorance to just suddenly up and leave it all behind.

The fact remains that the lies you tell yourself are damaging to your well-being. It's time to start listening to yourself. Before you justify your behavior, actions, or thoughts, look in deep and know the reason why. Are you being truthful to yourself, or are you covering up the unsavory facts?

Wounds can only be healed by honesty. And honesty requires emotional strength. Find that strength to open yourself up to new possibilities. Stop burying your head in the sand and sugar- coating your problems.

Create a personal mission statement

Your mission statement serves as a roadmap to where you are going and how you are going to get there. It is a concise list of your goals (whether short or long-term) and priorities that guide your day-to-day decision-making, by providing you your personal set of core values or principles.

Your mission statement is also a steady reminder that keeps you in check. A guiding light to your destination. It keeps you in the right frame of mind, as you will be allocating your resources in a way that is consistent with your goals. Although the process might be challenging, developing one is satisfying, challenging, and illuminating.

It's tempting to discard long-term goals in favor of the short-term ones. But by creating a personal mission statement, you can classify your most important beliefs and values, and reflect on how they affect your long-term goals. So you are able to readjust your everyday actions and priorities, find your deepest truths, and answer your greatest doubts.

It's necessary to always refresh your mission statement to keep the progress flowing. With one, you can better manage your time and say no to things to distractions.

Building a solid mission statement might take days. To create one, you need to be introspective, you need to reflect, review, and revise. You have to capture your true essence concisely.

Of course, a mission statement comes from deep self-assessment. You need to commit time toward examining your goals, values, passions, regrets, and limitations.

As well as a mission, you need a vision. You need to imagine. Envision your life in two, five, ten years from now. For instance, visualize the end of your current career. What achievements, contributions do you wish to have me in your field?

Put everything in writing. From the cluster, consider and pick the cherished few that best embody your values and character.

The key thing about a personal mission statement is that it is personal. It must be unique to you alone, not tailored to a second party's demands.

Your language in writing has to be specific, decisive and concrete, not watered-down. Use your "I will" and "I want" effectively. Take your action verbs seriously and also personalize your declarations. You can start each sentence with "I" to take ownership of your content.

Ultimately, you will come up with a cohesive piece that exemplifies your innermost goals that become your mission statement.

Always plan ahead

According to Confucius, the Chinese philosopher, a man who does not plan long ahead will find trouble at his door. Proper planning saves a lot of time on execution. The better you plan, the easier and more efficient you will get things done. It's a great investment and the reward will be a superior outcome in less time required for execution.

If you want to achieve a goal, execute a project, or fulfill a vision, always plan ahead. A bright future is a planned future. When you plan, you bring the future into the present and feel more in control of your daily life.

On the financial front, planning ahead saves you from unforeseen costs and traps. It saves a lot of headaches along the way. Imagine the stress of last-minute damage control. Imagine the pain of correcting a big error that could have been avoided at the infancy of the project.

Moreover, when you plan ahead, you stay in the moment. You are more aware of your own time. You are in charge of your own life. And you stay true to your own word. Lack of planning has led to many missed deadlines, meetings, including forgotten promises and failed businesses. To plan is to be accountable to yourself.

The biggest brands today have one thing in common: they prepare for the unexpected. Bring that level of awareness to life. Make plans for things like taxes, car repair, sick days, accidents, etc. A plan can change risk into an opportunity and a rewarding experience. If you don't anticipate risks or hard times, you can never respond to them effectively. Save money for contingencies and you will be glad you did.

When you plan, you become more productive. And because you are equipped with a clear action plan, you get more done in less time. Your performance improves. Life becomes less stressful as your productivity increases. Hence, you have time to grow. At the same time, taking risks is a criterion for growth. You have to expand your comfort zone to achieve success—but only with proper planning.

Whatever you do in life, never forget to assess the risks and opportunities. With planning, you can beat the competition because you are more emboldened to take the risks others won't. The fact remains that success is short-lived without risks. Learn to identify risks, weigh and sort them out with a laid-out plan.

When you plan, you become more proactive and less reactive. The way you respond to adversity changes. You don't just react for the sake of reacting. You take the initiative every single time.

Stop multitasking: one task at a time

Multitasking is outdated. Yet people still do ten things at once hoping to increase productivity. While software advancement has made multi-tasking easier, you should not be tempted to work with ten different technologies at a time.

You are more efficient and achieve better results if you focus on one task at a time. A good idea is to allocate a specific time for a certain task to be completed.

Even science says multitasking is stressful to your everyday life, affecting your productivity, motivation, and mood negatively. You can't properly control your memory, pay attention, or easily switch from task to another if you are constantly flooded with different electronic information.

Your brain doesn't like multitasking. Even if you pride yourself on being able to do so, your mind is never really focused. It's like meeting someone new in a crowded party—if you are distracted, you will forget that person's name.

A lack of concentration affects your professional life as well as your personal relationships and experiences. A distracted mind is not really living in the present—a mind that cannot effectively connect to coworkers, clients, family or friends.

Keep in mind that more tasks mean more mistakes. Lessened focus is a major attribute of multitasking. If you are juggling ten things at once, all you have is a divided mind that would naturally multiply mistakes. You won't be quick to filter out irrelevant information. To matters worse, you stand the chance of mental cross-firing and overlapping between tasks. If you hate mistakes, separately pay full attention.

If you continually multitask, you will eventually kill your memory. Science agrees that jumping from one task to another can cause you short-term memory, which is bound to worsen as you age. So if you are crushing it right now, know in five or ten years you could lose your touch.

Another major problem of multitasking is anxiety. If your attention is divided, you are more tensed and stressed. Anxiety closes down the frontal lobe of the brain adapted for creativity and critical thinking and creativity. Multitasking kills your creativity. If you devote your attention to too many things at once, coming up with new concepts and ideas becomes hard—as you don't even have enough working memory to be really creative. While you may complete your assignment, the results would only be average, never greater than your reach.

You are just wasting your time when you try to juggle too many tasks at once. A distracted mind trying to complete a large task alongside small ones is only shedding off precious time. The mind, in this case, would painfully and constantly need to reset and refocus, thus cutting off flow. If your mind is not flowing, you can't be productive. It's like enjoying a good movie or book—time flies sweetly.

A journey of a thousand miles

Chinese philosopher Lao Tzu said:"*The journey of a thousand miles begins with one step.*" It is so extremely important to take this first step. Once this is done, of course, you have to have the endurance and commitment and discipline to continue this journey, but you have to acknowledge the importance of this very first step and keep the momentum of it.

Every goal requires that first foot forward. You can just wait for things to happen. Initiatives and actions rule this world. You need to visualize more. Take action in changing a certain habit.

From cleaning up your room to making a call about that job opening to learning a new language, the first step matters. The "right" moment many never come. The "right" mood or circumstance many never appear. Most times, self-doubt is the real enemy.

Confidence and motivation are solidified by actions. A step in the right direction comes with both. It's quite alluring to remain in a daydream. But success is for dreamers who act, not daydreamers who fantasize.

We live in a world filled with endless possibilities. But also a world of difficulties and rejections. As adults, we fear failure more than we would like to admit. We can just blindly jump into things, without seriously thinking of the repercussions. We dread the thought of exploring strange grounds, of venturing into new businesses, of starting a new relationship, of trying out something new.

Because everything seems so daunting, you actually don't know where to begin. You take a look at that CEO, that musician, that scientist, and wonder if you could ever be like them. "It's impossible," your subconscious tells you, "and it's just beyond your control."

Remember that a journey of a thousand miles begins with a single step.

And the truth is that the mindsets of a doer and that of a daydreamer are different from each other. Every man and woman on the face of the earth is a bundle of ideas and talents. However, about less than percent only actually act on those ideas and talents. Self-doubt always manages to creep in to dissolve every spark of inspiration.

Know that successful people aren't necessary superhuman. They start small and move on to bigger things. Where others see stagnancy, they see a learning opportunity.

Want to get fit? Start small with few stretches and walks. Want to write that book? Jot down 100 words a day. Just start with something simple. A first step and you will own this journey called life.

Carpe diem: give your best every single day

Carpe diem is a Latin phrase that means "*seize the day*": to live life to the fullest, to suck all the marrow out of life. It's the most fantastic decision you can ever make. Life is happening right now. So it's up to you to mindfully feel the responsibility to make the best of it.

However, seizing the moment means more. It means not wasting a single opportunity. It means letting go of all the resistance as well as giving your all.

We make convenient excuses for not seizing the moment. We feel we don't have enough money, skill, self-esteem, preparation, or courage to take on the world. We procrastinate because we fear. But the time is now. Not tomorrow when you are more rested, not next week when you will feel more ready. Find that courage to completely say yes to life.

Bring your best to the table. Don't settle for anything else. You are your biggest motivator only when you have the highest expectations of yourself.

Whatever you do and wherever you are, be there fully. Live consciously and be present. Give your full attention, align yourself with the flow of nature.

Don't be scared of showing how you really feel to those you care for. Tell them you love them. Show it now. Don't wait for the next birthday, anniversary, or Christmas.

Life is all about giving and taking. But the trick to receiving is simply giving without nothing in return. Give love to get love. Provide value to make money. To get trust, be trustworthy yourself.

Just do it. Don't waste time second-guessing yourself. Missed opportunities are common than you think. Be bold. Ask that girl or boy for a date, start a conversation. Ask for that promotion, demand for that job. Seize the day and take the initiative.

If you really want it, go for it. A learning experience is the worst thing that can happen to even do better the next time.

Dare to dream and act on that dream. Let no one dictate what you are, what you can or cannot do. Plan ahead by using your goals to lay down your personal vision.

Be your authentic self. Be you. Don't wear a mask to water down your authenticity. Be real to yourself as well as others.

In the end, to seize the day means to wake up to all the incredible opportunities around you, to take action on those chances, and to bring your dreams into fulfillment.

CONCLUSION

Being self-disciplined is hard work, I know. But in the face of adversity, try to see any failure as a chance for a new start. See it as the beginning of something great: a chance to break out of your comfort zones and even take quantum leaps.

With an optimistic mindset, you can learn from your failures, pick up the shattered pieces, and move on to greater things. Life has taught us that failure is the father of greatness.

In whatever you choose to be self-disciplined in, make sure that it aligns with your true north, your passion. Then tap into your inner self and focus on what brings you satisfaction and motivation. Once you are aligned with your passion, everything else falls in place and things will start to move. Once you put in the right energy, the seed of self-control will grow into a sapling. And as you water, it will grow into a tree.

You cannot fool yourself into discipline. You have to address your challenges head-on and drown out the noise of distraction. Real clarity is possible when you see every problem as an opportunity in disguise; so attack the situation from all angles, and continuously question the root of the problem.

Before we part ways, I want to leave you with two final lessons from this book. But before that, let me say that this is a fascinating journey we are on. What makes it so interesting is that we are given so many chances to live life as we want to. You can create your own lifestyle, experience a transformation, or make choices that take you in a completely new direction. You are as free as you want to be. By challenging the fear and doing what scares you, failure no longer has any power over you. You can gain strength from the power of thought, confidence, and pushing your self-control to new levels.

Lesson #1: Understand your flaws

This is a book on self-improvement. Just take note that self-development doesn't mean self-perfection. We all have flaws. It's okay. You've lived with these flaws up until now, and that is okay too. With this book I hope that you can overcome and manage some of your flaws; other flaws we cannot change, or they may take more time to heal.

There is no big hurry. You have time. One day at a time and you'll make it. You can accept yourself, as you are, flaws and golden points. You might feel awkward or ashamed. But what are your good points? What makes you unique and valuable? List these out and remind yourself what they are.

Lesson #2: Always take your action

Nothing will happen to your self-control, and in turn, your life, unless you make the changes. To do this you have to be focused on the changes you want to see happen in your life as the result of your choices. Do you want to stay trapped or break free? Will you explore the unknowns of your real self, or stay hidden behind a veil of fear that keeps you doing the same thing over and over again? Will you take action or wait for the action to be taken against you?

The key to creating lasting change is to do something repetitively over a long time. It is the same with building habits. Do something for a few weeks and you'll gain some momentum, but if you stop, the habit you are trying to replace will return. You can start to transform your life today by taking some small action daily. Ask for something you want and take a small risk.

Do it for yourself. Do what you've always wanted to do but lacked the courage to move forward. Know that you can do anything you want to do if you dare to take action. Assess where you are at in your life and take that first step forward. Just one step will do. For today. Small steps are big gains over time. You've got this, now.